CLASSIFYING REALITY

Ratio Book Series

Each book in the series is devoted to a philosophical topic of particular contemporary interest, and features invited contributions from leading authorities in the chosen field.

Volumes published so far:

Classifying Reality, edited by David S. Oderberg
Developing Deontology: New Essays in Ethical Theory, edited by Brad Hooker
Agents and Their Actions, edited by Maximilian de Gaynesford
Philosophy of Literature, edited by Severin Schroeder
Essays on Derek Parfit's On What Matters, edited by Jussi Suikkanen and John Cottingham
Justice, Equality and Constructivism, edited by Brian Feltham
Wittgenstein and Reason, edited by John Preston
The Meaning of Theism, edited by John Cottingham
Metaphysics in Science, edited by Alice Drewery
The Self?, edited by Galen Strawson
On What We Owe to Each Other, edited by Philip Stratton-Lake
The Philosophy of Body, edited by Mike Proudfoot
Meaning and Representation, edited by Emma Borg
Arguing with Derrida, edited by Simon Glendinning
Normativity, edited by Jonathan Dancy

CLASSIFYING REALITY

Edited by
DAVID S. ODERBERG

WILEY-BLACKWELL

A John Wiley & Sons, Ltd., Publication

This edition first published 2013
Originally published as Volume 25, Issue 4 of *Ratio*
Chapters © 2013 The Authors
Book compilation © 2013 Blackwell Publishing Ltd

Blackwell Publishing was acquired by John Wiley & Sons in February 2007. Blackwell's publishing program has been merged with Wiley's global Scientific, Technical, and Medical business to form Wiley-Blackwell.

Registered Office
John Wiley & Sons Ltd, The Atrium, Southern Gate, Chichester, West Sussex, PO19 8SQ, United Kingdom

Editorial Offices
350 Main Street, Malden, MA 02148-5020, USA
9600 Garsington Road, Oxford, OX4 2DQ, UK
The Atrium, Southern Gate, Chichester, West Sussex, PO19 8SQ, UK

For details of our global editorial offices, for customer services, and for information about how to apply for permission to reuse the copyright material in this book please see our website at www.wiley.com/wiley-blackwell.

The right of David S. Oderberg to be identified as the authors of the editorial material in this work has been asserted in accordance with the UK Copyright, Designs and Patents Act 1988.

Library of Congress Cataloging-in-Publication Data

Classifying reality / edited by David S. Oderberg.
  pages cm
Includes bibliographical references and index.
ISBN 978-1-118-50835-0 (pbk.)
  1. Reality. 2. Classification. 3. Categories (Philosophy) 4. Science–Philosophy.
I. Oderberg, David S., editor of compilation.
  BD331.C53 2013
  001.01′2–dc23
                                2013001459

A catalogue record for this book is available from the British Library.

Cover design by Design Deluxe

Set in 11 on 12 pt New Baskerville by Toppan Best-set Premedia Limited
Printed in Malaysia by Ho Printing (M) Sdn Bhd

1   2013

CONTENTS

Notes on Contributors   vii

Introduction   1

1   Categorial Predication   5
    E. J. Lowe

2   Nature's Joints: A Realistic Defence of Natural
    Properties   23
    D. H. Mellor

3   Boundaries in Reality   41
    Tuomas E. Tahko

4   Contrastive Explanations in Evolutionary Biology   61
    Stephen Boulter

5   Animate Beings: Their Nature and Identity   79
    Gary S. Rosenkrantz

6   Classifying Processes: An Essay in Applied Ontology   101
    Barry Smith

Index   127

NOTES ON CONTRIBUTORS

Stephen Boulter　　　Oxford Brookes University

E. J. Lowe　　　Durham University

D. H. Mellor　　　University of Cambridge

Gary S. Rosenkrantz　University of North Carolina at Greensboro

Barry Smith　　　University at Buffalo

Tuomas E. Tahko　　University of Helsinki

INTRODUCTION

Is reality classifiable? In other words, does it have boundaries or 'joints' that enable us to assign various categories to its different constituents? If not, on what might one base a negative answer? If reality can be classified, how should we classify it? Further, how might classification problems show up in the special sciences?

One might, of course, propose that reality can be classified but that this entails nothing about its having any objective lineaments. One might even claim that there are multiple possible classifications, all consistent and all somehow imposed on an otherwise amorphous reality by the human mind. Philosophical opinion, as on so many issues, ranges from the highly sceptical to the strongly realist. Recent years have seen a revival of metaphysical thinking that, for all the disagreements among its partisans, is clearly realist when it comes to categories and boundaries in reality. Whether inspired by Aristotle, by natural science pure and simple, or by the neo-essentialism of Kripke/Putnam semantics, these metaphysicians are generally committed to the existence of a mind-independent world that comes to us pre-packaged, so to speak, and awaiting classification through one or both of relatively a priori philosophical reflection and the a posteriori investigations of natural science.

In this book, six philosophers on the realist side of the classification question bring diverse considerations to bear upon it. The essays are roughly divided into the first three, which concentrate on general issues relevant to the defence of a realistic approach, and the latter three, which defend objective classification in biology. It should be no surprise that biology looms large: this is due to the by-now received view that before Darwinism took hold, the classification of species involved sharp, fixed boundaries and unique answers; whereas the age of evolutionism has involved support for the fluidity of species classification and the lack of unique answers to 'what is it?'-type questions concerning how a species finds its taxonomic place. For all that this picture of the history of biology and its philosophy is somewhat simplistic, there can be no doubt that biology is still the battleground on which philosophical debates over classification are most commonly fought.

As for the more general papers, Jonathan Lowe takes on the task of evaluating whether formal logic should itself be aligned with the objective categories of ontology. Castigating modern Fregean logic for the problems with which it saddles itself – notoriously, the status of the concept *horse* – Lowe urges that we set aside the 'constraints of a particular style of logical formalism and the ramshackle ontology that typically accompanies it.' Instead, we need to 'sort out our *ontology* properly first, and only then shape our formal logic to fit it, not vice versa'. Lowe then draws on Aristotelian categorial ontology to set out a new way of formalising predication, with separate terms for primary substances (ontologically independent particulars), secondary substances (kinds), attributes (universals) and modes (property instances). The resulting basic system looks very different from what we are used to, but it may be, as Lowe implies, that contemporary metaphysics has indeed been in thrall to an ontological shadow cast by a particular, and historically comparatively recent, way of formalising the subject-predicate relation.

Hugh Mellor sets out to defend the idea that nature not only has objective joints, but those joints are sharp and not a matter of degree. He criticizes the Fregean thought that properties are no more than functions from objects to truth values: 'why not let our ontology include both functions and objects?' Nor is there anything in Tarski's theory of truth to justify his belief in the reality of objects but not of properties. Quine, too, fails to impugn the reality of properties (beyond their identity with their extensions). For Mellor, there are natural properties that are 'independent of minds and languages'. Moreover, there is no need to postulate (as David Lewis does) properties that are 'less than perfectly natural' (such as a disjunctive property with perfectly natural properties as disjuncts), since they serve no role in explaining the objective resemblances between things that is not already performed by laws of nature with disjunctive antecedents.

Tuomas Tahko takes on several conventionalist arguments against natural boundaries in reality. One is that there are too many differences in the world to allow for anything but a stipulated boundary between kinds of entity; in other words, nature does not force upon us one set of boundaries rather than another, but with no principled way of deciding between them, so that any decision must be purely stipulative. A second argument is to the effect that the classifications we make are grounded in our psychological biases, no matter how regular these are across time and space. A third argument is that since different species, given their varying mental and physical characteristics, almost certainly 'carve up nature' in different ways, there can be no unique, privileged way of doing so. Tahko's response is to insist that even if we do not (and maybe cannot) know all the boundaries in reality, if we focus on one case – for instance, fundamental physical particles – the realist can undermine conventionalism. Macroscopic objects depend on physical particles, and these particles have exact properties (even if in some cases the properties have an essential probabilistic element). Stipulated ('fiat') entities have only contingent exact properties, whereas at least some of those belonging to fundamental particles are necessary. By developing this reasoning, Tahko argues that the conventionalist objections to realism can be refuted.

Moving on to more applied issues, Stephen Boulter is concerned with contrastive explanations in biology. Here, the biologist tries to explain why a certain organism or organismic trait exists rather than some other. Why are the non-actualised alternatives not what we see in nature? Some forms will be possible but for some contingent reason non-actual; others will be non-actual because logically, metaphysically, physically or biologically impossible. (Why are there no flying pigs? This is in fact an important question in the philosophy of biology.) But how are the various possibilities to be grounded, especially if we are to have a theory that would make an impression on a biologist? Finding the usual contemporary approaches to modality unsatisfactory, Boulter proposes a return to Aristotelian themes. Here, the emphasis is on the powers of organisms as grounded in their natures: 'it is an entity's nature which sets the boundaries of possibility for it because a nature is ultimately a set of powers and liabilities.' In an even more Aristotelian vein, '[i]n the biological case, all real biological possibilities are ontologically grounded in the essences of actual forms.' The epistemology of relative possibility, then, 'reduces to the epistemology of essences'. Needless to say, biological essentialism is hardly at the centre of most current thinking in philosophy of biology, but it is having something of a revival and will, for Boulter, point both philosophers and biologists in the right direction for devising plausible contrastive explanations.

Gary Rosenkrantz takes up a theme he has explored before – the provision of logically necessary and sufficient conditions for something's being a living thing. To this he adds an account of the identity conditions of carbon-based organisms. Again, the inspiration comes from Aristotle, with the emphasis being on metabolic and (for some living beings) psychological activity. Rosenkrantz argues that life necessarily involves at least one of these, which entails that viruses are inanimate. To produce sufficient conditions, he appeals to the concept of goal-directed activity, itself reducible to non-teleological features of natural selection. Weaving together goal-directedness, metabolism, and psychological activity, Rosenkrantz proposes necessary and sufficient conditions not just for living beings in the broad sense, but conditions enabling a distinction between living beings and their parts. For carbon-based life, he argues that we need also to appeal to the concept of a master-part – vital, essential, and regulative of the organism. It is the master-part that secures the persistence of a carbon-based organism over time.

At an even more specific level, Barry Smith focuses on the use of formal ontology in the classification of processes, in particular biological processes – as important to biologists as the usual work on species. Smith outlines a system that uses the vocabulary familiar to practising scientists (gene, cell, receptor, membrane, for example) – designed to unify the theoretical and experimental ends of the biological spectrum. He also sketches Basic Formal Ontology, a system whose terms (entity, continuant, occurrent, quality, etc.) are more familiar to metaphysicians than scientists. Processes are occurrents – four-dimensional entities with temporal parts, and ontologically dependent on the continuants that participate in them. They are changes but do not themselves change. Using many detailed examples of typical biological processes, Smith then provides the basic features of a taxonomy that is both metaphysically and scientifically satisfying, and likely to be of use in various fields, such as the development of computer algorithms for diagnostic purposes.

Together, these essays provide a fascinating insight into the ways in which realist philosophers, in particular those who derive inspiration from Aristotle, approach problems of classification at both the theoretical and applied ends of ontology.

1

CATEGORIAL PREDICATION

E. J. Lowe

Abstract
When, for example, we say of something that it 'is an object', or 'is an event', or 'is a property', we are engaging in *categorial predication*: we are assigning something to a certain *ontological category*. Ontological categorization is clearly a type of classification, but it differs radically from the types of classification that are involved in the taxonomic practices of empirical sciences, as when a physicist says of a certain particle that it 'is an electron', or when a zoologist says of a certain animal that it 'is a mammal', or when a meteorologist says of a certain weather-phenomenon that it 'is a hurricane'. Classifications of the latter types presuppose that the items being classified have already been assigned to appropriate ontological categories, such as the categories of *object, species,* or *event.* What do categorial predications *mean?* How are their *truth-conditions* to be determined, and how can those truth-conditions be known to be satisfied? Do they have *truthmakers?* Questions like these are amongst those addressed in the present chapter.

1. Fantology; or, 'Ontology Lite'

Most philosophers today who have been brought up in the analytical tradition have been exposed, at a formative period of their thinking, to the formalism of first-order predicate logic with identity. This has equipped them with a certain conception of reference and predication which is, from the point of view of serious ontology, extremely thin and superficial. It is a view which embodies – to invoke Barry Smith's apt term[1] – all the myths of 'Fantology': the idea that the most basic form of atomic proposition is one that may be symbolized as '*Fa*', where '*F*' is the predicate and '*a*' is a singular term, or 'individual constant' (the logical counterpart of a proper name). The only further elaboration of this

---

[1]   See Barry Smith, 'Of Substances, Accidents and Universals: In Defence of a Constituent Ontology', *Philosophical Papers* 26 (1997), pp. 105–27, and 'Against Fantology', in M. E. Reicher and J. C. Marek (eds), *Experience and Analysis* (Vienna: HPT&ÖBV, 2005).

Classifying Reality, First Edition. Edited by David S. Oderberg. Copyright © 2013 The Authors. Book compilation © 2013 Blackwell Publishing Ltd.

that is countenanced is to admit *relational* predicates with any finite number, *n*, of 'places', giving us as the most general form of an atomic proposition '$R^n a_1 a_2 \ldots a_n$'. And the only 'relation' that is given any special formal recognition is the dyadic relation of *identity*, with its own dedicated symbol, '=', as in '$a_1 = a_2$'. Sometimes, a formal recognition is also accorded to the monadic *existence* predicate, as in 'E!a', but this is generally analysed in terms of the particular (or, more tendentiously, 'existential') quantifier, '∃', together with identity, as being equivalent to '$(\exists x)(x = a)$'. And that, basically, is the sum total of the formal machinery of standard predicate logic that serves to represent anything remotely 'ontological' in character: it is 'Ontology Lite'.

One point I am aiming to make here is that there are many more ontological distinctions that we need to be able to make that go beyond either the distinction between object (or 'individual') and property or that between existence and identity. It just isn't good enough to say, with W. V. Quine, that the fundamental question of ontology is 'What is there?', and that its most concise answer is 'Everything'.[2] Ontology is concerned above all with the *categorial* structure of reality – the division of reality into fundamental *types* of entity and their ontological relations with one another. The object/property distinction is very probably *one* such distinction that any system of categorial ontology should recognize, and identity is *one* such relation, but very plausibly there are many others besides these.

Note that, on the now standard view – basically Quine's, which is a development of Frege's and Russell's – we don't even get an 'ontological commitment' to *properties and relations* out of 'first-order' languages, since the latter don't involve quantification into predicate position. For that we need, supposedly, a *second*-order language, where we can say things of the form '$(\exists F)(Fa)$' and the like. But this then apparently treats 'properties' (the 'values' of second-order variables) as second-order *objects*, of which yet higher order properties may further be predicated. So, on this view, the object/property distinction is really just a *relative* one, with an nth-order *object* being an $(n-1)^{th}$-order *property*, for all $n > 1$. Hence, *all* entities are 'objects' on this view, but there are different 'orders' of objects, starting with first-order ones which are not 'properties' of anything. And maybe we can even discern an echo here, however weak, of the Aristotelian notion of a 'primary substance', which is not 'said of' anything – of which much more anon. (Quine himself, of course, was sceptical about including 'properties' in our ontology – at least, properties conceived as 'universals', as opposed to items identifiable as *sets* of first-order objects – on the grounds that he could see no principled way to *individuate* them, rendering them vulnerable to his dictum 'No entity without identity'.)

The next pernicious aspect of the 'standard' view is this: it accommodates no notion of 'property' other than as *something* – though exactly *what* is often left obscure – that 'corresponds' to a *predicate*, as in '*Fa*', where '*F*' supposedly expresses a 'property' of *a*. This is despite the fact that we know that, on pain of contradiction, not *every* predicate can denote or express a property – this simply being a consequence of one version of Russell's paradox. Take the predicate '– is non-self-exemplifying', which seemingly applies, for example, to the first-order property of *being green* ('first-order' property because it is a property of first-order *objects*, such as *apples* and *leaves*). 'Being green (greenness) is not *green*' certainly seems to be true, whence it seems that we can conclude that 'Being green is *non-self-exemplifying*' is also true. If the example is not liked, another can easily replace it. But we know that there can be no (second-order) *property* (property of a first-order property) of *being non-self-exemplifying*, since if there were it could plainly be *neither* self-exemplifying *nor* non-self-exemplifying, giving us a contradiction.

We are also now in the territory of Frege's notorious paradox of the concept (that is, first-order property) *horse*, which he contended was *not* an object because it is not 'saturated' – the apparent implication being that the *object* that we *do* denote by the singular term '(the property of) being a *horse*' is not what is expressed by the predicate '– is a horse'.[3] The best that the standard view can do at this point, it seems, is to say that for every 'property' of order *n* – 'property' in the sense of *semantic value of a predicate* – there is a corresponding *proxy*-object of order $(n + 1)$, which is the semantic value of a corresponding singular term. If that is right, then it turns out that the object/property distinction

[3] See Gottlob Frege, 'On Concept and Object', in *Translations from the Philosophical Writings of Gottlob Frege*, 2nd edn, ed. and trans. P. T. Geach and M. Black (Oxford: Blackwell, 1960).

isn't even straightforwardly *relative*, as was suggested earlier. Rather, we have a series of *objects* of ascending 'orders' and, *distinct but in parallel with that*, a series of corresponding 'properties'. The scheme is something like the following – where, listed in each column of the table, are typical expressions whose semantic values are the 'objects' and 'properties' of successively higher 'orders':

	Objects	**Properties**
1st order	'Dobbin'	'– is a horse'
2nd order	'Being a horse'	'– is a first-order property'
3rd order	'Being a first-order property'	'– is a second-order property'
4th order	'Being a second-order property'	'– is a third-order property'
Et cetera		

This scheme is organized so as to enable us, supposedly, to assign appropriate 'semantic values' to the semantically interpretable parts (subjects and predicates) of sentences such as the following:

(1) Dobbin is a horse.
(2) Being a horse is a first-order property.
(3) Being a first-order property is a second-order property.
Et cetera

Of course, as well as affirming, for example, (2) – 'Being a horse is a *first-order property*' – we are *also* supposed to be able to affirm 'Being a horse is a *second-order object*', since the foregoing table displays that alleged fact by listing 'Being a horse' in the second row under the 'Objects' column. One might suppose that this would entitle us to conclude that *a first-order property is (identical with) a second-order object*: but that is problematic, given Frege's contention that the object/property (or object/concept) distinction is mutually exclusive, on the grounds that properties but not objects are 'unsaturated' entities. This just shows how intractable the 'paradox' is, at least given Fregean assumptions.

But what, really, are the 'semantic values' of predicates – *properties* – supposed to *be*? On one view – not Frege's, clearly, but maybe Quine's – they are just the 'extensions' of those predicates: the sets of things to which they apply, such as the set of all (actually existing) horses in the case of the predicate '– is a horse'. This would make the semantic value of that predicate an *object*, however, since sets are pretty clearly objects by any reasonable account. On another view – neither Frege's nor Quine's – the semantic value of such a predicate is instead a certain kind of *function*: namely, a function from 'possible worlds' to sets of objects existing in those worlds.[4] Thus, the semantic value of the predicate '– is a horse', on this view, is a function from possible worlds to the sets of *horses* existing in those worlds (and Quine would reject the view because he rejects 'possible worlds'). This, in the current technical jargon, assigns an *intension*, rather than just an *extension*, as the 'semantic value' of this predicate. But, fairly evidently, a 'function', at least as this is normally understood by mathematical logicians, is itself just a special kind of set-theoretical entity and so a certain kind of *abstract object* – not the kind of 'unsaturated' entity that Frege took properties (or 'concepts') to be. However, these entanglements take us too far from our current purpose, save to illustrate once more the baroque qualities of 'Fantology' and its insouciance about questions of serious ontology. Its adherents exhibit no genuine interest in understanding the real *nature* of properties, if such entities there be.

However, one important further application of the foregoing scheme of objects and properties of different 'orders' is worth mentioning, and it concerns the notion of *existence*. As was indicated earlier, 'Dobbin exists' is standardly analysed as '$(\exists x)(x = \text{Dobbin})$', and here '$(\exists x)(x = -)$' may be regarded as denoting or expressing a *first*-order property – the property, possessed by Dobbin and indeed by all other existing objects, of *being identical with something*. But we can, supposedly, also *re-parse* '$(\exists x)(x = \text{Dobbin})$' by treating the expression '= Dobbin' as being, in effect, a sign for the quite different first-order property of *being identical with Dobbin*. This being done, '$(\exists x)(x -)$' may then be

[4]   Frege himself does, in his own way, treat properties ('concepts') as functions, but as functions from objects to *truth-values*, and he accordingly regards functions as 'unsaturated' entities: see 'Function and Concept', in Geach and Black (eds), *Translations from the Philosophical Works of Gottlob Frege*. Russell speaks instead of 'propositional functions', conceived as functions from objects to *propositions*: see 'Propositional Functions', in Bertrand Russell, *Introduction to Mathematical Philosophy* (London: George Allen and Unwin, 1919). But neither view is any more attractive than the views now under discussion in this paragraph.

taken to express the *second*-order property of *having at least one (first-order) instance*, which is here being predicated of the first-order property of being identical with Dobbin. Thus re-parsed, '($\exists x$)(x = Dobbin)' should really be understood as having the logical form '$G_2(F_1)$', with 'F_1' denoting the first-order property of being identical with Dobbin and 'G_2' the second-order property of having at least one instance, so that the whole sentence may be re-translated into (rather barbaric) English as 'Being identical with Dobbin has at least one instance'. But once again, of course, the singular term 'being identical with Dobbin' now has to be taken to denote a second-order *object*, not the first-order *property* that is the semantic value of the predicate '– is identical with Dobbin', at least if we follow Frege in these matters.

Now, at this point I want to cry out that all of this is completely *insane* from an ontological point of view that aspires to any seriousness, being driven entirely by the constraints of a particular style of logical formalism and the ramshackle ontology that typically accompanies it. We need to sort out our *ontology* properly first, and only then shape our formal logic to fit it, not vice versa. And the first step towards sanity here is to abandon the idea that there is something special and sacrosanct about the 'atomic' logical form 'Fa' – Fantology. Fantology, which originates from the systems of formal logic newly developed by Frege and Russell around the beginning of the twentieth century, does implicitly rest on certain ontological assumptions, but on rather weak and ill-thought-out ones – assumptions which seemed to matter little when they were overshadowed by the sheer *logical* power of those formal systems. It weakly reflects, thus, the *object/property* distinction, whose historical roots lie in traditional Aristotelian substance ontology – ultimately, in fact, in Aristotle's early work, the *Categories*.[5] But in the *Categories*, Aristotle does not assume a simple dichotomy between 'substance' (or 'object') and 'property'. Rather, he introduces a more complex *four-fold* ontological scheme by way of two key formal notions: those of 'being *said of* a subject' and 'being *in* a subject'. Somewhat obscure though these notions may initially seem to be, on further investigation they in fact bear rich ontological fruit and valuable insights into the

5   See Aristotle, *Categories and De Interpretatione*, trans. J. L. Ackrill (Oxford: Clarendon Press, 1963).

proper relations between logic and ontology. It is a worthwhile
project, then, to try to clarify them in terms rather more familiar
to present-day metaphysicians, whereupon a comparison between
Fantology and traditional Aristotelian categorial ontology will
prove to be quite revealing.

2. Aristotelian Categorial Ontology and Its Logical Formalization

I turn now to the foregoing task: that of explicating the 'being
said of'/ 'being in' distinction and its application by Aristotle in
his characterizations of the most basic ontological types figuring
in his four-fold categorial scheme, these types being (1) *primary
substance*, (2) *secondary substance*, (3) *property* or *attribute* and (4)
individual accident or *mode* (to use some familiar Scholastic nomen-
clature). First of all, then, being *said of* is clearly indicative of
predication, while being *in* is indicative of what would, long after
Aristotle's time, come to be called *inherence*. Now, Aristotle's
primary substances in the *Categories* are described by him as being
neither said of nor in a subject – in other words, they are not
predicable of anything, nor do they exist 'in' anything as ontological ingredients or constituents. Being neither 'of' nor 'in' other
things, they are thus in neither sense ontologically *dependent*
beings, and this indeed is why primary substances are taken by
him to be the entities that are ontologically most fundamental. By
contrast, Aristotle's *secondary* substances – the species and genera
of primary substances – are, according to him, 'said of' but not
'in' a subject, thus sharing one kind of ontological independence
with primary substances but not another. Thus, for example, in
affirming that Dobbin *is a horse*, we are predicating *the species horse*
of the primary or individual substance Dobbin. But, on Aristotle's
view, this species isn't 'in' the individual substance, as an ontological 'constituent' of the latter – that is, as some entity numerically *distinct* from that substance but one which, nonetheless,
somehow helps to *constitute* it as the particular substance that it is.
Next, we have items in the category 'both said of and in a subject',
which gives us a contrast between the predicate '– is a horse' and,
say, the predicate '– is warm-blooded'. The latter expresses a
property or *attribute* of Dobbin, which he shares with all other
individual substances of the same species (all other horses) –
shares, it seems, as an ingredient or constituent in his *nature or*

being (his 'essence').[6] Finally, there are the items that are '*in* a subject but not *said of* a subject', which are generally taken to be a primary substance's 'individual accidents' or 'modes' – items such as the *particular* whiteness of Dobbin, as opposed both to the *universal* whiteness that he shares with all other white primary substances and also to the particular whitenesses of *other* white primary substances.

It will be noted that all *predicables* belong either to the category of secondary substances or to the category of attributes and that all items in these categories are *universals* rather than particulars – all *particulars* belonging either to the category of primary substances or to the category of modes. Thus, on this account, although modes are in one sense 'properties' of primary substances, they are not *predicable* of them, which may sound odd to the ears of present-day metaphysicians. And yet it does seem to be borne out by what we actually *say* in English and other natural languages. When, for instance, we say that Dobbin *is white*, we are making no reference to his *individual* whiteness, even if it is *because* this individual whiteness 'inheres' in him that whiteness (the universal) is predicable of him. (Incidentally, it is precisely because present-day metaphysics is equivocal about the status of 'properties', sometimes treating them as universals and some-times as particulars in the guise of 'tropes', that I generally prefer to use the term 'attribute' to denote items that are 'both said of and in a subject'.)

Much more can and should be said about all this, but already we can see that we have here a much richer ontology than anything that is offered by Fantology and one that is, despite being categorially more complex, ontologically far less baroque and extravagant. For example, we have no grounds now for believing in a potentially infinite hierarchy of 'orders' of objects and properties. Thus, warm-bloodedness is *said of* a subject – it is a 'predicable' – but is not *itself* a subject, in the relevant sense of 'subject'. Of course, the *word* 'warm-bloodedness' can be made the *grammatical* 'subject' of a *verb*: but that is not the *ontological* conception

---

[6]   Here I am, for the sake of simplicity, glossing over an important distinction between properties in the strictest sense, which are necessarily shared by all primary substances of the same species – by all individual horses, for instance – and what might be called 'general accidents', which are shared by some but not all such primary substances, an example being Dobbin's whiteness (since not all horses are white). I take it that, for the Aristotelian, both warm-bloodedness and whiteness are 'in' Dobbin, but only the former is *necessarily* 'in' *all* individual horses.

of a subject, which is that of a *substance* (whether primary or secondary). So, the sentence 'Warm-bloodedness is a property of horses', say, shouldn't be understood as predicating the (pseudo-) property or attribute of *being a property of horses* of the (pseudo-) subject *warm-bloodedness*. Rather, it is just a roundabout way of saying 'Horses are warm-blooded', which expresses a general truth about the secondary substance or species *horse*, holding in virtue of that species' *essence*. To regard warm-bloodedness as a *subject* – a quasi-substance – would simply and literally be a *category mistake*, on the Aristotelian view. Thus, on this approach, we need have no truck with 'second-order logic' (at least as it is ordinarily conceived) and other such formal monstrosities. And we aren't faced with Frege's hideous 'paradox' of the concept *horse*. For that paradox is really just an artefact of an impoverished logical formalism and its misconceived ontological assumptions.

So, what would a *better* logical formalism look like? First of all, if we are going to follow the Aristotle of the *Categories*, we shall obviously need *four* distinct classes of 'material' (that is, non-formal or non-logical) expressions, not just the *two* ('*F*' and '*a*') of standard first-order predicate logic, in order to denote (1) primary substances, (2) secondary substances, (3) properties or attributes and (4) individual accidents or modes. Let us then adopt the following notation for this purpose:

(1) $a, b, c, \ldots$ denote primary substances.
(2) $\alpha, \beta, \gamma, \ldots$ denote secondary substances.
(3) $F, G, H, \ldots$ denote attributes.
(4) $\mu, \nu, \xi, \ldots$ denote modes.

Again, if we are going to follow the Aristotle of the *Categories*, we need *different* devices for expressing 'saying of' (predication) and 'being in' (inherence), in place of the *single* device for expressing 'predication' that we find in standard first-order logic. And indeed I am happy to follow Aristotle here too, partly for purposes of illustration, but also because I largely agree with him.[7] So, to

---

[7] See my *The Four-Category Ontology: A Metaphysical Foundation for Natural Science* (Oxford: Clarendon Press, 2006). Although I broadly follow Aristotle in that book, I do not there deploy his being said of/being in distinction, preferring instead to make use of a three-way distinction between instantiation, characterization and exemplification. I still prefer the latter approach, but am using this opportunity to explore further an approach that is closer to Aristotle's own.

this end, let us simply use *post*-positioning to represent *predication*, as in standard first-order logic, giving us, for example, 'β*a*' and '*Fa*' as ways to symbolize 'Dobbin is a horse' and 'Dobbin is warm-blooded' respectively (where 'β' = 'horse', '*a*' = 'Dobbin' and '*F*' = 'warm-blooded'). And let us additionally use *pre*-positioning to represent *inherence*, giving us, for example, '*a*μ' and '*a*G' as ways to symbolize 'This whiteness is in Dobbin' and 'Whiteness is in Dobbin' respectively (where 'μ' = 'this whiteness', '*a*' = Dobbin and '*G*' = 'white(ness)'). Note that, with this scheme, we can represent 'Dobbin is white' and 'Whiteness is in Dobbin' as '*Ga*' and '*a*G' respectively, reversing the positions of '*G*' and '*a*'. But, very plausibly, two such sentences are *logically equivalent*, even if they are not synonymous, so that for logical purposes we may discard formulas of the form '*a*G' as superfluous. Here is the scheme laid out in tabular form, followed by the formation rules for constructing 'atomic' sentences:

1. Subjects	2. Predicables	3. Inherents
Primary substances	Secondary substances	Attributes
a, *b*, *c*, . . .	α, β, γ, . . .	*F*, *G*, *H*, . . .
Secondary substances	Attributes	Modes
α, β, γ, . . .	*F*, *G*, *H*, . . .	μ, ν, ξ, . . .

Rule 1. Any item in column 1 can have something in column 2 *predicated* of it, this being represented by *post*-positioning the former item to the latter: thus, 'β*a*', '*Ga*', 'αβ' and '*F*α' – as in 'Dobbin is a horse', 'Dobbin is white', 'Horses are mammals' (or 'A/The horse is a mammal') and 'Mammals are warm-blooded', where 'β' = 'horse', '*a*' = 'Dobbin', '*G*' = 'white', 'α' = 'mammal' and '*F*' = 'warm-blooded'. (Note that the definite or indefinite article in 'A/The horse is a mammal' is logically redundant and would not, of course, have any equivalent in Latin and many other languages.)

Rule 2. Any item in column 1 can have something in column 3 *inherent* in it, this being represented by *pre*-positioning the former item to the latter: thus, '*a*G', '*a*μ', 'α*F*' and 'βμ' – as in 'White-(ness) is in Dobbin', 'This whiteness is in Dobbin', 'Warm-blooded(ness) is in mammals' and 'This whiteness is in horses', where '*G*' = 'white(ness)', '*a*' = 'Dobbin', 'μ' = 'this whiteness', '*F*' = 'warm-blooded(ness)', 'α' = 'mammal' and 'β' = 'horse'. As implied above, we take 'warm-blooded' and 'warm-blooded*ness*' to be equivalent for ontological purposes, the difference in form being merely a grammatical peculiarity of English. And, once more, we take 'White(ness) is in Dobbin' and 'Warm-blooded(ness) is in mammals' to be logically equivalent, respectively, to 'Dobbin is white' and 'Mammals are warm-blooded', rendering formulas of the forms 'aG' and 'αF' redundant for logical purposes. The only odd case is the last, 'This whiteness is in horses', for how, it might be asked, can a *mode* 'inhere' in a *species*? One answer might be that it does so just as long as *some* individual member of the species, such as Dobbin, has this whiteness inhering in him. Alternatively, we might simply want to rule out this last case as not well-formed and restrict accordingly the formation rule stated at the beginning of this paragraph.

Observe that these formation rules give us just the following *six* types of 'atomic' sentences: Fa, αb, $G\beta$, $\alpha\beta$, $a\mu$ and αv. The first type predicates an attribute of a primary substance, the second predicates a secondary substance of a primary substance, the third predicates an attribute of a secondary substance, the fourth predicates a secondary substance of another secondary substance, the fifth expresses the inherence of a mode in a primary substance and the sixth expresses the inherence of a mode in a secondary substance. (For reasons just explained, the first type also serves to express the inherence of an attribute in a primary substance and the third type also serves to express the inherence of an attribute in a secondary substance.) As just mentioned, we might want to exclude the sixth type and allow only the first five. There is nothing sacrosanct, of course, about this notation, and others could have been used quite as well. But it is interesting to note that, if we restrict our attention to just the first five types, we can see that the four basic classes of 'material' terms occur in them with the following frequencies: secondary substance terms (α, β) *four* times, primary substance terms (a, b) *three* times, attribute terms (F, G) *two* times and mode terms (μ, v) just *once*. Whether that rather neat distribution has any significance is hard to say. In saying that just these types of atomic sentences are well-formed, other combinations of terms are by implication excluded, such as 'GF' and '$\mu\beta$': one attribute cannot be predicated of or inhere in another attribute, nor can a mode be predicated of a secondary substance or a secondary substance inhere in a mode.

Of course, this gives us, so far, only a way to formally represent 'atomic' propositions. There is a lot more expressive power that we still need to cater for in order to express, for instance, truths of *existence* and *identity*. Here we may follow existing practice, however, and use the symbols 'E!' and '=' respectively for these purposes. But we also need *quantifiers* – at least a *particular* and a *universal* quantifier – although for this purpose too we may as well again follow existing practice and use the symbols '∃' and '∀'. However, we shall *not* adopt the usual assumption that existence can be 'analysed' in terms of '∃' and '='. And another appropriate diversion from standard practice would be to favour so-called *restricted* quantifiers for most purposes. For instance, in order to represent the sentence 'Some (individual) horses are white', we shall use a formula such as '(∃x: αx) (Fx)', where 'α' = 'horse' and 'F' = 'white'. Similarly, in order to represent the sentence 'Some (species of) mammals are viviparous', we shall use a formula such as '(∃φ: βφ) (Gφ)', where 'β' = 'mammal' and 'G' = 'viviparous'. (It will be noticed, incidentally, that I am here adopting the convention of using x, y, z, . . . as variables ranging over primary substances and φ, χ, ψ, . . . as variables ranging over secondary substances.)

My reason for favouring restricted quantifiers for these purposes emerges most clearly in the case of universal generalizations. Consider, for instance, the true sentence 'All (species of) mammals are warm-blooded'. This I prefer to represent by a formula such as '(∀φ: βφ) (Hφ)', where 'β' = 'mammal' and 'H' = 'warm-blooded'. This, I think, is greatly preferable to a formula such as '(∀φ) (βφ → Hφ)', which uses *unrestricted* quantification over secondary substances. In fairly plain English, the difference is, very roughly, between 'Any mammalian species is warm-blooded' and 'Any species, if it is mammalian, is warm-blooded'. But one problem with the latter formulation arises when we consider what sort of sentence qualifies as an *instance* of this sort of generalization. The sort of sentence that qualifies is one such as 'If (the species) mountain is mammalian, then it is warm-blooded' – or, more colloquially, 'If mountains are mammals, then they are warm-blooded' – which I would represent by a formula such as '(βγ → Hγ)', where 'γ' = 'mountain'. The latter clearly *is* entailed by '(∀φ) (βφ → Hφ)', by an application of the logical rule of universal instantiation. But the *antecedent* of 'If mountains are mammals, then they are warm-blooded' – 'Mountains are mammals' – is very hard to make any sense of. Indeed, it seems to constitute a *category* mistake: not, indeed, one involving the four *most basic* categories of the Aristotelian scheme, but one involving two different *sub*-categories of secondary substances.

Mammals (that is, mammalian *species*, such as the horse and the rabbit) belong to the sub-category of *biological* species, whereas mountains belong to the sub-category of *geological* species – and it apparently makes no sense even to entertain the 'thought' that mountains are mammals, that is, that a species of geological structure is a species of living organism. No such absurdity is entailed by my preferred formula, '($\forall \phi$: $\beta \phi$) ($H\phi$)'. This, *in conjunction with* a formula of the form '$\beta \gamma$', entails one of the form '$H\gamma$'. For instance, 'All (species of) mammals are warm-blooded' together with 'The horse is a (species of) mammal' entails 'The horse is warm-blooded'. But the additional premise here, 'The horse is a (species of) mammal', is evidently perfectly uncontentious and indeed just expresses an essential truth about horses.

I noted above in passing that I follow the convention of using x, y, z, . . . as variables ranging over primary substances and ϕ, χ, ψ, . . . as variables ranging over secondary substances. For the sake of completeness, however, we need also variables ranging over *attributes* and *modes*. But in saying this we must be careful to remember that the latter are not *subjects* (that is, they are not *substances*, either primary or secondary). We can have *names* for them and *variables* ranging over them, but that should not lead us to treat them as quasi- or pseudo-substances, which is the implicit mistake of those philosophers and logicians who think that 'second-order' logic, by quantifying into predicate position, incurs ontological commitment to a new class of 'objects', over and above the 'first-order' objects that are the supposed values of 'first-order' variables. This, I think, is just a horrible ontological muddle on their part. *Properties*, in the form of both attributes (universal properties) and modes (particular properties), should certainly be accorded a place in any sensible ontology, but it is wrong to *reify* or *hypostatize* them. This is because they are essentially 'inherent' entities, always being 'in' a subject (substance) – or, as we might otherwise put it, always being only *aspects* of substances, or '*ways* substances are', never substances in their own right.

Note, incidentally, that the formal logical language sketched above is in fact only classifiable as a '*first*-order' language in the standard sense, despite the fact that it includes names for and variables ranging over properties, in the shape of both attributes and modes. This is because it does *not* involve 'quantification into predicate position' in the standard sense. (Moreover, in model-theoretic terms, it does not invoke a domain which includes *all sub-sets* of the domain of first-order objects quantified over by a standard first-order language and hence a domain whose cardinality is necessarily greater than that of the latter, even if there are infinitely many such first-order objects; a domain of quantification for a formalized language like mine could perfectly well include only a denumerable infinity of entities, so long as it included some entities belonging to each of the four basic ontological categories.) Now, the latter phenomenon – quantification into predicate position – is exemplified in a formula of so-called 'second-order' logic such as '$(\exists F)(Fa)$'. But, in standard predicate logic, the '*F*' in '*Fa*' is supposed to represent a *predicate*, understood as an 'incomplete' expression such as '– is white'. By contrast, '*Fa*' in my formalization of Aristotelian categorial ontology serves to express the proposition that the attribute *F*(ness) inheres in, or is predicable of, the primary substance *a*. '*F*' and '*a*' here are thus to be thought of as two *terms*, each *naming* an entity belonging to a certain ontological category. In standard predicate logic, '*F*' is not a *term* in this sense at all, since it doesn't serve to *name* any entity but just represents what remains of a complete predicative sentence when a name is removed from it – as, for example, '– is white' is what remains when the name 'Dobbin' is removed from the sentence 'Dobbin is white'. Another way to make this point is to say that, in the standard formalism, the '*F*' in '*Fa*' has an implicit 'is' of predication *built into it*, whereas in my formalism '*F*' simply denotes a certain *attribute* and its predicability of *a* is represented formally not by a further symbol (although this could certainly be done), but rather by means of the post-positioning convention whereby '*a*' is placed immediately after '*F*'.

3. Categorial Predication: Its Form, Meaning and Use

I come now properly to the topic indicated by the title of this chapter, *categorial predication*, for which the preceding two sections have provided a necessary preliminary. The system of formal logic whose language I have been constructing is meant to be one which respects and reflects certain fundamental categorial distinctions of an ontological nature. But now we have to consider how we can speak *explicitly* of such categorial distinctions, by extending the expressive power of our formalized language. So far, these categorial distinctions have been only *implicit* in the language, being embodied in our choice of *symbol* types and our ways of representing predication and inherence. A *categorial* statement, however, will be one which explicitly assigns some entity to a specific ontological category; and in our present system, of course, we have *four* such categories: those of *primary* and *secondary sub-stance, attribute* and *mode*. (But we should again recall that these are just the *basic* categories of the system, which need by no means exclude further *sub-*categories of these basic ones.)

So consider, for example, a statement such as 'Dobbin is a primary substance', or 'The horse is a secondary substance (species)'. On the face of it, the expression '– is a primary sub-stance' is a *predicate*, which *says something* of Dobbin. (That, as we have seen, is at least the now standard conception of what a 'predicate' is.) But on our currently preferred *Aristotelian* view of predication, *predicables* are what are 'sayable' of subjects. So, does there not exist a *predicable* that is said of Dobbin by the statement 'Dobbin is a primary substance'? If so, then that predicable will have to be either a *secondary substance* or else an *attribute*: for these and only these are things that may be 'said of' a subject. One suggestion, then, might be that there is a species (or, rather, a very high-level *genus*) – that of *primary substance* – which can be 'said of' Dobbin, very much as the species *horse* and the genus *mammal* can be 'said of' Dobbin. An alternative suggestion is that there is a highly abstract *attribute* – that of *being a primary substance* – which can be 'said of' Dobbin, very much as the attributes *being warm-blooded* and *being viviparous* can be 'said of' Dobbin. But neither suggestion is preferable to the other and both are in fact unat-tractive (and perhaps even incoherent).[8]

The solution is to reject *both* suggestions. This, however, requires us to recognize a certain ambiguity in the notion of 'saying of' or predication. In one sense – the sense hitherto to the fore in our discussion of the Aristotelian system – the notion of predication is a *relational* one. In this sense, in predication *one* thing is 'said of' *another* thing, with each of these things belonging to an appropriate ontological category. For example, an *attribute* is said of a *substance*, either primary or secondary. Or a *secondary substance* is said of a *primary substance*. Or *one* secondary substance is said of *another* secondary substance. But then there is and must

---

[8]   Consider, thus, the proposal that 'primary substance' denotes a *genus* to which all primary substances belong. Then it turns out that, since all genera belong to the category of *secondary* substance, the sentence 'Primary substance is a secondary substance' must be in some sense true. But I find it very hard to make any clear sense of this.

be another, *non*-relational notion of 'saying of' or predication, where this includes assigning an item to a certain ontological category. (Another plausible case is that of predicating *existence* of something, since it is highly doubtful that existence is properly conceived as a *property* or *attribute* of anything; if it were, then it ought to make sense to say that *existence exists*, and yet it scarcely does seem to make sense to say this.)

One characteristic of a statement involving categorial predication is that if it is 'formally correct', then it should be *necessarily true*. A perspicuous formalized language should respect this requirement. Suppose, thus, that we introduce the formal ontological predicates 'P', 'S', 'A' and 'M' into the formalized language that was developed in section II. These are to express, respectively, the English predicates '– is a primary substance', '– is a secondary substance', '– is an attribute' and '– is a mode'. Then, to distinguish *categorial* predication from (what we might aptly call) *material* predication (which we have chosen to express by the device of post-positioning), let us use *superscription* for the former. Thus, for example, 'Dobbin is a primary substance' will be formalized as 'a^P', where 'a' represents 'Dobbin'. And then our point is that such a statement will be necessarily true if and only if it is *well-formed*, as it is in this case: that is, it will be necessarily true if and only if the categorial superscript matches the symbol-type to which it is attached. In the present case, 'a' is a symbol for an individual or primary substance and hence matches the superscript 'P'. By contrast, a formula such as 'F^P', representing a statement such as 'Whiteness is a primary substance', is just *not well-formed* in this system and hence *necessarily false*.

But how, it might now be asked, could there be any real *use* for such statements of categorial predication, given that the categorial distinctions are already built into the symbolism of the formalized language (as they are not, perhaps, in a natural language such as English)? The answer is that we want our language to be capable of talking about *pure ontology*. For that, we need also names and variables which are *categorially neutral*, in order to say things such as 'Every primary substance has at least one mode inherent in it'. Thus, using 'e' (for 'entity') as a new type of ontologically neutral variable, we could express the last-mentioned sentence formally in this manner: '$(\forall e_1)(e_1{}^P \rightarrow (\exists e_2)(e_2{}^M \ \& \ e_1 e_2))$'. (Here we are using unrestricted quantifiers, of course, and the proposal would be that these are *only* to be used in statements of pure ontology; note also that, in the formula just stated, '$e_1 e_2$' must be construed as expressing *inherence* rather than predication, given the formation rules and the typing of e_1 and e_2 as P and M respectively.) Statements of pure ontology would all be like this and in this way we could envisage the construction of a formal, axiomatizable *theory* of pure ontology, which would constitute an a priori science analogous to various branches of pure mathematics. In the formal theory of pure ontology, no *specific* entity of any category would be referred to, such as *Dobbin* or *whiteness*: all statements would concern the categories themselves and relationships obtaining between their members purely in virtue of their categorial status, as in the case of the sample statement cited above. Of course, for present purposes I am assuming that the 'correct' formal theory of pure ontology will be a characteristically 'Aristotelian' one, of the kind sketched earlier. But that assumption is not vital to the notion of pure ontology as such. Indeed, one can envisage alternative (or even just *different*) systems of pure ontology, just as there are different branches of pure mathematics. (Some systems of ontology, for instance, include the basic category of *event*, whereas in the 'Aristotelian' ontology there is no room for such entities save in the guise, perhaps, of modes of primary substances.) However, one should not take the analogy with pure mathematics too far, since the latter consists of theories which do make reference to *specific* entities of certain types, such as the natural numbers, whereas pure ontology is perfectly general or 'topic neutral' in its subject matter.

To repeat an earlier point of great importance, categorial predications are – as Wittgenstein might at one time have remarked – true, when they are true, simply in virtue of their 'logical grammar'. Thus, 'a^P' can be seen to be true simply by inspection of its logical form. In that sense, such a truth has and requires no 'truthmaker', if by a 'truthmaker' we mean some *entity* which, by existing, *makes* it true. 'a^P' doesn't even require the existence of the primary or individual substance a to make it true: thus, 'Dobbin is a primary substance' can be known to be a true – indeed, a *necessarily* true – categorial predication *whether or not* Dobbin is known to exist. I do want to allow, of course, that from 'a^P' we may validly infer '$(\exists e)(e^P \ \& \ e = a)$', and vice versa. Thus, I happy to allow that 'Some primary substance is (identical with) Dobbin' is just a longwinded way of saying 'Dobbin is a primary substance'. But recall that I am rejecting the claim that 'Some primary substance is (identical with) Dobbin' is logically equivalent to 'Dobbin *exists* and is a primary substance' or, more generally, that '$(\exists e)(e^P \ \& \ e = a)$' is logically equivalent to '$(E!a \ \& \ a^P)$'.

Dobbin's existing is no doubt logically equivalent to some *existing* primary substance's being (identical with) Dobbin, but not just to *Dobbin's being a primary substance*, since the latter is just an a priori truth arising from an ontological necessity concerning the correct ontological categorization of any such item as Dobbin is *conceived* to be, whether or not Dobbin actually *exists.*[9]

[9]   I am grateful for comments received when an earlier version of this essay was presented at the *Ratio* Conference on Classifying Reality, held at the University of Reading in May 2011. I should also like to thank David Oderberg for very helpful remarks on the penultimate draft.

2

NATURE'S JOINTS: A REALISTIC DEFENCE OF
NATURAL PROPERTIES

D. H. Mellor

Abstract
This chapter attacks two contrary views. One denies that nature has
joints, taking the properties we call natural to be merely artefacts of
our theories. The other accepts real natural properties but takes
their naturalness to come by degrees. I argue that both are wrong:
natural properties are real, and their naturalness no more comes
by degrees than does the naturalness of the things that have
them.[1]

1. Introduction

In 1939 G. E. Moore claimed to prove the existence of an external
world by proving that he had two hands.[2] His conclusion is less
contentious than his proof, despite Peter van Inwagen's claim that
'there was never any such thing as Descartes's left leg' nor therefore, presumably, any such things as Moore's hands.[3] Fortunately
Moore's case does not rest solely on his hands. He lists several
other 'things outside of us' (as he puts it): 'a shoe and sock . . . a
sheet of paper and a human hand . . . two sheets of paper';[4] and
nowhere suggests that it is harder to prove that they (and many
other things, including the whole organisms van Inwagen does
believe in) exist than that his hands do.

However, my interest here is not in the soundness of Moore's
argument but in some implications of the fact that, despite an
external world needing only one thing 'outside of us', all his
examples are of *pairs* of things. These examples imply that a pair

---

[1]   My revisions of the first version of this chapter, given to a Ratio conference at the
University of Reading on 7 May 2011, owe much to comments on it made then and later,
and especially to those of Anthony Fisher and David Oderberg.
[2]   G. E. Moore, 'Proof of an External World' [1939], in his *Philosophical Papers* (London:
George Allen & Unwin, 1959), pp. 145–6.
[3]   Peter van Inwagen, *Ontology, Identity, and Modality* (Cambridge: Cambridge University
Press, 2001), p. 82.
[4]   Moore, 'External World', p. 145.

of hands differs from a pair of sheets of paper, that both these pairs differ from a hand and a sheet of paper, and that any of these three pairs could exist without the other two. (Proving that a pair of hands exists does not prove that a hand and a sheet of paper exist.) So Moore could have concluded, although he didn't, not just that there are two external things – hands – but that those things differ in kind from shoes, socks, sheets of paper and other things 'outside of us'.

Of course what distinguishes things of these kinds depends partly on what we mean by 'hands', 'shoes', 'socks' and 'sheets of paper', and that is more or less up to us. What is not up to us, as David Lewis says, is whether a thing *is* a hand, shoe, etc., so understood:[5] whether, for example, things have whatever properties, known or unknown, make them sheets of paper and not hands, i.e. things we can write *on* but not *with*. In this chapter I argue for the reality of these properties, against two contrary views. One is that nature has no joints, and that what we call natural properties are just imaginary counterparts of our best theories' predicates. The other is that just as, in Orwell's *Animal Farm*, all animals are equal but some are more equal than others, so in reality, while nature's joints are all natural, some are more natural than others. I shall tackle these two theses in turn, starting with the thesis that nature has no language-independent (or mind-independent) properties.

2. Natural Properties

Paradigms of what I mean by 'natural properties' are the sizes, shapes, masses and temperatures of planets, people, shoes, atoms, etc. – and the distances between them, since for brevity I shall call relations 'properties' too. By 'natural' I shall mean 'contingent and factual', i.e. not counting necessary properties like self-identity, or being a prime number, or moral and aesthetic properties like being good or being ugly.

Natural properties, so understood, are those that Lewis calls 'sparse', meaning that they 'ground the objective resemblances

---

[5]   David Lewis, 'New Work for a Theory of Universals' [1983], in his *Papers in Metaphysics and Epistemology* (Cambridge: Cambridge University Press, 1999), p. 47.

and the causal powers of things',[6] and thereby give nature the joints that I, Plato,[7] and others say it has. In most of what follows I shall restrict the term 'property' to these, partly again for brevity but mainly to exclude Lewis's 'gerrymandered and miscellaneous' classes,[8] which he only calls properties because they 'need not be classes of *actual* things' (my italics).[9] That seems to me a poor reason to call such classes 'properties' when that term is more widely and usefully used for (what groups things into) collections that are, in some respects, *not* miscellaneous.

Take Moore's hands. Hands need surfaces, not only to give them the shapes and other properties they need in order to be hands, but also to give them identities, i.e. to make them countable things, distinct from their surroundings, and from each other. But surfaces can only do this by separating entities with different properties: in this case those that make hands solid and those that make their surroundings – air, water, etc. – fluid. Without the properties that give nature surfaces, there would be no countable natural particulars.

Why then are these properties more contentious than the particulars whose identities they enable? What properties there are is a good question, as is whether the answer to that question is given by microphysics alone or by all natural sciences. And neither question can arise unless there are properties as well as the particulars to which we ascribe them. Why might we doubt that?

3. Objections to Properties

I start with Hilary Putnam's Derridean claim that 'we interpret our languages or nothing does',[10] i.e. that nothing 'outside of us' constrains what our theories are about. Putnam's argument for this is that stating an external constraint on what a theory is about merely extends the theory, whose extended form we can then always interpret so as to make it come out true. If that were so, then believing '*a* is *F*' could not entail believing either in the

---

[6]   'New Work', p. 12.
[7]   Plato, 'Phaedrus', trans. Alexander Nehemas and Paul Woodruff, in his *Complete Works*, ed. John M Cooper (Indianapolis: Hackett, 1997).
[8]   'New Work', p. 12.
[9]   p. 10.
[10] Hilary Putnam, 'Models and Reality', *Journal of Symbolic Logic* 45 (1980), p. 482.

particular a or in the property F. But it is not so, for Lewis's reason: for if it is up to us what we mean by 'F' and 'a', part of what we choose to mean by those terms may be, and usually is, that it is not up to us whether a thing satisfies 'F', and is what 'a' refers to. Given what we actually mean by 'Moore' and 'hand', nothing can be what 'Moore's hands' refer to that lacks the properties which make them what we call 'hands' and parts of what we call 'Moore'. The fact that we could have made the word 'Moore' mean Russell and the word 'hand' mean foot is irrelevant.

Moreover, for Putnam's sentence, 'we interpret our languages or nothing does', to mean anything, every token of its words, including those you have just read, must have whatever properties it takes to *be* a token of those words. And for any token of his sentence to mean what it does, the token first-person 'we' in it must refer to entities like us who (i) have whatever properties it takes to have a language and (ii) include whoever produced that very token. In short, we cannot both give Putnam's sentence the meaning he wants it to have and take it to be true. (Though even if we could, that would hardly matter here: for denying the exist-ence of language-independent things as well as their language-independent properties will not tell us why those properties are more contentious than the things that have them.)

Next, before tackling more specific objections to properties, I must emphasise that these do not include nominalism, in its non-Quinean sense of denying the existence of *universals*. That is because we need not, although I do, follow David Armstrong in taking properties to be universals:[11] sets of exactly resembl-ing tropes,[12] or particulars,[13] can also give nature language-independent joints. And while trope theorists and nominalists have problems (i) defending the modal realism needed to distin-guish actually co-extensive properties, like having a heart and having kidneys, and (ii) saying what resemblance is, if not a uni-versal,[14] these do not stop them crediting things with properties.

Still, there *are* real objections to properties, which I do need to rebut. I start with Frege's thesis that properties (which he calls

[11] David Armstrong, *Universals and Scientific Realism* (Cambridge: Cambridge University Press, 1978).

[12] D. C. Williams, 'On the Elements of Being: I' [1953], in *Properties*, ed. D. H. Mellor and Alex Oliver (Oxford: Oxford University Press, 1997).

[13] Gonzalo Rodriguez-Pereyra, *Resemblance Nominalism* (Oxford: Clarendon Press, 2002).

[14] See Bertrand Russell, 'On Our Knowledge of Universals' [1912], in his *The Problems of Philosophy* (Oxford: Oxford University Press, 1959), and Chris Daly, 'Tropes', in *Properties*.

'concepts') are not 'objects', because (i) they are functions whose value, when the particulars that have them are their arguments, is the truth-value True, and (ii)

> an object is anything that is not a function, so that an expression for it does *not* contain any empty place'.[15]

So for Frege, if m is Moore's right hand, the property H of being a hand is a function whose value is True when its argument is m. And while the name 'm' in the sentence 'm is H' is complete, the predicate '. . . is H' is not, since it has an empty place that needs filling with a term like 'm' to complete a sentence with a truth value.

But why does calling properties 'functions' rather than 'objects' show that there are none: why not let our ontology include both functions and objects? The reason is that any predicate 'F' in a true or false sentence 'm is F' generates a Fregean function from m to a truth-value. These functions are not confined to what, for reasons given in §2, I mean by 'properties': namely contingent and factual entities that 'ground the objective resemblances and the causal powers of things'. They are also generated by predicates like '. . . contingent', '. . . prime', '. . . non-existent', none of which correspond to the natural properties that give nature its joints.

In short, Frege's functions are just gratuitous duplications of predicates: they tell us nothing about natural properties. They do not even tell us how properties, natural or not, differ from the particulars that have them. For if 'm is H' can be decomposed into a complete 'm' and an incomplete '. . . is H', it can equally well be decomposed into a complete 'H' and an incomplete 'm is . . .', where the singular term is what has the empty place that needs filling with a complete term like 'H'. In other words, if H is a function, from particulars to truth values, m is also a function, from properties to truth values. Frege's treatment of particulars as objects, and properties as functions, rather than the other way round, expresses a prejudice that his theory does nothing to justify.

The same goes for Tarski's theory of truth, which postulates no properties at all, merely particulars and the predicates they

---

[15] Gottlob Frege, 'Function and Concept' [1891], trans. P. T. Geach, in *Properties*, p. 43.

'satisfy', i.e. which apply to them.[16] But if Tarski's theory does not tell us what makes the predicate 'H' apply to Moore's hands and not to his feet, at least it does not preclude the obvious answer that his hands have, and his feet lack, whatever properties make 'H' apply to them. (Nor does it preclude the same answer to the question of what makes the predicate 'is a token of "H" ' apply to some linguistic tokens and not others; and similarly for tokens of names, sentences and other linguistic types.)

This lacuna in Tarski's theory is not itself an objection to his starting with particulars instead of properties. But his theory no more justifies his doing so than Frege's does, as we can see by comparing his theory with my and Alex Oliver's tongue-in-cheek alternative, on which

'a is F' is true iff there is a φ such that 'is F' designates φ and 'a' falls under φ,

and which, as we say,

suggests that 'a is F' is only committed to F-ness, not to an entity designated by 'a'. And why not? If we can have a primitive semantic relation, *applies to*, relating predicates to entities designated by singular terms, why not another primitive relation, *falls under*, relating singular terms to entities designated by predicates?[17]

We do not of course recommend our alternative, which we give only to show that Tarski's theory, like Frege's, does nothing to justify its assumption that particulars are objects and properties are not.

Then there is Quine, for whom 'to be assumed as an entity is to be reckoned as the value of a variable'.[18] So for Quine, properties (which he calls 'attributes') exist if and only if we need second-order as well as first-order quantifiers in order to be able to state any empirical truth without using names or other referring terms. And we do need them, since quantitative laws, like Newton's

[16] Alfred Tarski, 'The Semantic Conception of Truth' [1944], in *Readings in Philosophical Analysis*, ed. Herbert Feigl and Wilfrid Sellars (New York: Appleton-Century-Crofts, 1949), p. 63.

[17] D. H. Mellor and Alex Oliver, 'Introduction', in *Properties*, p. 15.

[18] W. v. O. Quine, 'On What There Is' [1948], in *Properties*, p. 83.

second law of motion, quantify over determinate values of determinables like mass, force and acceleration. These Quine will accept, but only if they are identified with their extensions, i.e. with the classes of all the things that have them. His reason is that since 'physical objects are well individuated', so are classes of them, because their 'identity consists simply in the identity of the members'.[19] That is why he will not accept properties that are *not* classes of well-individuated physical objects, because they 'have no clear principle of individuation'.[20]

But Quine is wrong, for two reasons. First, many determinate properties are in fact better individuated than many of the objects that have them. Take the values of temperature, pressure and density whose continuous distributions across entities like whirlpools and storms explain their behaviour. These values – degrees Celsius, pounds per square inch, grams per litre – are far better individuated than the fluid regions over which, in such cases, they are distributed.

Second, laws of nature entail that many precise temperatures, pressures, masses, etc., have no actual instances at all. Statistical mechanics, for example, implies that no spatially extended thing has an absolutely precise temperature, even when in thermal equilibrium. The only actual class with which we could identify these temperatures is the null class, which would make all of them identical not only to each other but to all uninstantiated values of every other determinable. And as Quine is an actualist – because he cannot see how to individuate merely possible fat men in doorways[21] – he cannot escape this implication by identifying properties with the classes of all their *possible* instances, as Lewis does.[22] (This is also why Quine, unlike Lewis, cannot distinguish properties, like having a heart and having kidneys, which in our world are co-extensive.)

But could we not remove these ontological commitments of quantitative laws by reading their second-order quantifiers substitutionally instead of objectually? Perhaps we could, if there were only countably many different temperatures, masses, etc.; for then the rational numbers we use to distinguish them could give us

---

[19] Quine, 'On the Individuation of Attributes' [1975], in his *Theories and Things* (Cambridge, Mass.: Harvard University Press, 1981), p. 101.
[20] Quine, 'On the Individuation of Attributes', p. 101.
[21] 'On What There Is', p. 76.
[22] 'New Work', p. 10.

names for all of them. But why, even if we could, should we try to do this, when Quine's only reason for rejecting properties that are not classes – that they cannot be individuated as clearly as the objects that have them – is, as we have seen, false? This way of dispensing with properties would, like Frege's and Tarski's ways, only express a prejudice against them that it does nothing to justify.

In any case, the substitutional quantification trick will not work even if it is feasible, since it will not eliminate all references to determinate properties. In particular, it will not eliminate them from sentences saying *which* determinables they are determinates of. For example, as Frank Jackson observes, 'Red is a colour' cannot just mean that all red things are coloured, or even that, *necessarily*, all red things are coloured, since it is also necessary that all red things are shaped, and that they are extended.[23] Similarly for '100 grams is a mass', '100°C is a temperature', and so on. The fact is that Quine's extensional metaphysics can no more cope with the determinable properties of shaped and extended things than with the non-extensional physical probability statements entailed by sciences ranging from microphysics through genetics to epidemiology.

The only really serious problem generated by adding properties to particulars is F. H. Bradley's notorious regress.[24] For a particular *a* to have the property *F*, it cannot be enough for *a* and *F* to exist or *b*, which is not *F*, *would* be *F*. The particular *a* must also 'instantiate' *F*, which *b* does not. Yet adding an instantiation relation *I* to *a* and *F* will still not stop *b* being *F* unless *I* 'relates' *F* to *a* but not to *b*. But adding that relation will not work either, for the same reason; and so on, and so on – a seemingly vicious regress.

Whatever the answer to this regress, all I need say about it here is that each of the other theories I have mentioned generates it too. For *a* but not *b* to *fall under* a Fregean concept *F*, *a* and *F* must, and *b* and *F* must not, fall under the falling under concept; Tarski's *satisfaction* relation must relate *a* but not *b* to the predicate '. . . is *F*'; Quine's *class-membership* relation must relate *a* but not *b* to the class of *F*'s instances; Putnam's *interpret-as* relation must relate '*a*' and '*F*' to some pairs of entities but not to others; and so on. All theories of truth that postulate particulars generate these

---

[23]   Frank Jackson, 'Statements About Universals' [1977], in *Properties*, pp. 89–90.
[24]   F. H. Bradley, *Appearance and Reality*, 2nd ed. (Oxford: Clarendon Press, 1897), bk 1, ch. 2.

regresses – as indeed do theories of how 'concrete particulars and abstract universals are composed of tropes'.[25] In short, as we are all in Bradley's boat, and will sink or swim in it together, his regress gives us no reason to replace the apparent properties of objects with functions, predicates, classes or interpretations.

4. Properties and Particulars

Assuming then that there are properties, as well as particulars, that are independent of minds and languages, how do these two kinds of entity differ? I take their being independent of language to show that, as Ramsey says,

> the task on which we are engaged is not merely one of English grammar: we are not school children analysing sentences into subject, extensions of the subject, complement, and so on,[26]

and, specifically, that we cannot derive the distinction between particulars and properties from a subject-predicate distinction. Nor, as we have seen, can we derive it from Frege's object–function distinction, since, as Ramsey also says, a logician can

> take any type of objects whatever as the subject of his reasoning, and call them individuals, meaning by that simply that he has chosen this type to reason about, though he might equally have chosen any other type and called them individuals.[27]

So the real question I take to be this: why are the paradigms of what we call 'particulars' because they are what we quantify over first, i.e. take our *first*-order quantifiers to range over, what J. L. Austin calls 'moderate-sized specimens of dry goods'?[28] The obvious answer is that these goods, including ourselves (and our hands) have, as we have seen, causal boundaries that we can use to individuate them without having to know on *what* properties (of them and us) their boundaries, and our ability to detect them, depend.

---

[25] Williams, 'On the Elements of Being: I', p. 118.
[26] F. P. Ramsey, 'Universals' [1925], in *Properties*, p. 61.
[27] p. 72.
[28] J. L. Austin, *Sense & Sensibilia*, ed. G. J. Warnock (Oxford: Oxford University Press, 1962), p. 8.

This ability enables us to devise testable theories crediting us and other 'dry goods' with causal properties that explain how we resemble, differ from and interact with each other, properties whose distributions we can then use to mark subtler boundaries, like those of the swirling parts of whirlpools and storms. But then these particulars too, like the dry goods we start with, will occupy limited regions of spacetime – which is why we call natural particulars 'concrete' and the properties they can share with other particulars anywhere in spacetime 'abstract'.

In short, the difference between natural particulars and their properties lies in their different relations to space and time. Ramsey denies this, because he thinks that arguing about whether a table is a continuant or a property of events is not 'arguing about how many places the table can be in at once, but about its logical nature'.[29] Maybe so, but whatever a table *is* – a sequence of causally-related 'gen-identical' particulars,[30] a 'perduring' particular with temporal parts,[31] an enduring thing without temporal parts,[32] or 'a maximal sum of compresent tropes'[33] – it will still have the limited spacetime location that all natural particulars have (except perhaps the whole spacetime universe, and spacetime itself, if there are such things).

This limited location is what explains why natural particulars are less contentious than their properties. It does so because, if we are to quantify over any empirical entities other than facts, we must quantify over some entities *first*, i.e. use first-order quantifiers. And entities with spacetime boundaries are the only ones that we, as such entities, can individuate well enough to give our quantifiers definite domains without having previously individuated other entities. Whether, having done this, we also need to quantify over their properties, i.e. to use second-order quantifiers, is therefore bound to be a more contentious matter.

5. Properties and Laws

Granted, however, that we both can and should quantify over the contingent properties of natural particulars, what properties are

[29] 'Universals', p. 58.
[30] Hans Reichenbach, *The Philosophy of Space and Time*, trans. Maria Reichenbach and John Freund (New York: Dover, 1928).
[31] Lewis, *On the Plurality of Worlds*, pp. 202–4.
[32] Mellor, *Real Time II* (London: Routledge, 1998), ch. 8.2.
[33] Keith Campbell, 'The Metaphysic of Abstract Particulars' [1979], in *Properties*, p. 132.

there for these particulars to have? Since they are independent of language, we cannot expect an actual contingent predicate to correspond to each of them (though each will of course correspond to a *possible* predicate applying to all and only those particulars with that property). But for most actual predicates, I agree with Armstrong that (replacing his term 'universal' with 'property'),

> there may be none, one or many properties in virtue of which the predicate applies [and] given a property, there may be none, one or many predicates which apply in virtue of that property.[34]

Take red things, i.e. things to which the English predicate '. . . is red' applies, which include red light, red paint, red-hot objects and red filters. These are made to satisfy '. . . is red' by quite different properties: red light by its frequency range; red paint by the chemical composition of its surface; red-hot objects by their temperature, and red filters by their molecular structure.[35] There is no one property that makes entities of all these kinds red. It takes empirical investigation to discover the properties that make entities of various kinds red: which and how many they are is certainly not deducible from the meaning of 'red'.

But if our predicates will not tell us what properties there are, what will? Part of the answer is given by Sydney Shoemaker's thesis that properties are what determine the causal powers of things. Thus, in his example, a thing with the property of being knife-shaped that also has the property of being made of steel 'will have the power of cutting butter, cheese and wood, if applied to these substances with suitable pressure . . .'; and so on.[36] In other words, what fixes what properties there are is what causation there is. And that, I agree with Donald Davidson, is fixed by what laws of nature there are,[37] with two caveats. One is that, for me, the laws of nature include the probabilistic laws that Davidson overlooks. The other is that, like Armstrong,[38] what I mean by 'law of nature' is not a

---

[34] *Universals and Scientific Realism,* vol. II, p. 9.
[35] Mellor, 'Properties and Predicates' [1991], in *Properties,* p. 265.
[36] 'Causality and Properties' [1980], in *Properties,* p. 234.
[37] 'Causal Relations' [1967], in *Causation,* ed. Ernest Sosa and Michael Tooley (Oxford: Oxford University Press, 1993), p. 160.
[38] *What Is a Law of Nature?* (Cambridge: Cambridge University Press, 1983).

kind of statement (e.g. an unrestricted universal or statistical generalisation that supports counterfactuals), but whatever it is – whether a Humean regularity or something else – that makes that statement true.

But if the laws of nature, so understood, determine what natural properties there are, how do they do so? My answer is that these

> properties are identified *a posteriori* by scientific theories, construed as Ramsey sentences: i.e., as saying for example that there are properties *C*, *F* and *G* such that in *C*-circumstances all *F*-events have such-and-such a chance of being followed by *G*-events. If that statement is true, then there are such properties, and there is such a law, of which those properties are constituents. And being a constituent of some such laws is . . . all there is to being a property. There is no more to temperatures than the thermodynamic and other laws they occur in; no more to masses and forces than the laws of motion and of motion's gravitational and other causes; and so on. In other words, if we stated all the laws there are in a single Ramsey sentence Σ, the properties Σ would quantify over are all the properties there are.[39]

I call this thesis 'Ramsey's test', by analogy with 'Quine's test' for what particulars there are: namely, what our first-order quantifiers must range over to enable us to state any truth without using names or other singular terms. Similarly, by Ramsey's test, the natural properties that exist are those that our higher-order quantifiers must range over to enable us to state any law of nature without using predicates.

Having defended this thesis at length elsewhere,[40] I will only make two points about it here. First, Σ replaces *all* our theories' predicates with existentially quantified variables, not just the predicates which theories introduce in order to explain observable facts that we could state without using those predicates. This is because, unlike Ramsey, I am not using his sentences as an

[39] 'Properties and Predicates', p. 260.
[40] *The Facts of Causation* (London: Routledge, 1995), ch. 15, §§4–7.

alternative to defining theoretical predicates in observable terms,[41] but to say what properties, observable or not, our theories say there are.

Second, Ramsey's test does not 'entail that we can ever know or even express Σ, merely that the properties our world contains are those which Σ would need to quantify over if it *were* expressed'.[42] And this definition is not really hypothetical, any more than is Ramsey's theory of laws, as what, if we had a deductive system of everything, would be axioms of it. For here as there, as Ramsey says, 'the . . . if is only a spurious one; what is asserted is simply something about the whole world',[43] in my case that it contains all and only those properties needed to make Σ true.

6. Ramsey's Test

Ramsey's test is controversial, partly because it rules out complex properties. These, if F and G are properties, are properties like $F \vee G$, which everything is that is F *or* G, $\neg F$, which everything is that is *not* F, and $F \wedge G$, which everything is that is F *and* G. To see why the test excludes these, take the two stable isotopes of chlorine, ^{35}Cl and ^{37}Cl, which differ physically but not chemically, and let F be the property of being ^{35}Cl and G the property of being ^{37}Cl. Now suppose there is also the complex property $F \vee G$, of being 'stable chlorine'. Then by Ramsey's test, the Ramsey sentence Σ must quantify over $F \vee G$. So $F \vee G$ must occur in some law, e.g. in the antecedents of the laws of chlorine chemistry. But then, for $F \vee G$ to be complex, i.e. for those laws to apply to ^{35}Cl and ^{37}Cl, they must also contain F and contain G, which must then be distinguished by occurring separately in other laws, as they do in those of each isotope's distinctive physics. But then Σ must quantify over F and over G; in which case it need not also quantify over $F \vee G$.

This is why, by Ramsey's test, there are no disjunctive properties, merely laws, like those of chlorine chemistry, with disjunctive antecedents or consequents; and similarly for negative properties. These however are not the implications that make Ramsey's a

---

[41] 'Theories' [1929], in his *Philosophical Papers*, ed. D. H. Mellor (Cambridge: Cambridge University Press, 1990).

[42] *The Facts of Causation*, p. 193.

[43] 'Universals of Law and of Fact' [1928], in his *Philosophical Papers*, §14.

controversial test for properties which, in Lewis's words, 'ground the objective resemblances and the causal powers of things'. For if, for example, neither a nor b has the property F, say of being ^{35}Cl, this does not entail that they have another property, $\neg F$, which makes them resemble each other in some other way. They may resemble each other, e.g. if a and b are both sodium, or they may not, e.g. if a is oxygen and b is lead. This is why no one who believes in language-independent properties thinks the existence of a property F makes $\neg F$ a property too, even if that of the predicate '. . . is F' makes '. . . is $\neg F$' a predicate.

Similarly with disjunctive properties. If F and G are properties, and a is F and b is G, they may, or may not, resemble each other. They will if F and G are the same property, or are compatible, e.g. if F is a mass and G is a temperature, and a is G as well as F. But if F and G are *in*compatible, e.g. if they are different masses, then a and b will not resemble each other in that respect, and may not do so in any other. This is why no one thinks that satisfying the disjunctive predicate '. . . is $F \vee G$' is enough to make a and b resemble each other by making them share the disjunctive property $F \vee G$.

What makes Ramsey's test contentious is that it rules out *conjunctive* properties. The objection to its doing this is not that two things that share two properties F and G must also share a third, $F \wedge G$, in order to resemble each other: no one thinks that. Those who believe in conjunctive properties, as Armstrong does, offer two quite different arguments for them.[44]

Armstrong's first argument is that 'it is logically and epistemically possible that all properties are conjunctive', i.e. that no properties are simple.[45] For example, just as chlorine turns out to be a mixture of atoms with different properties, so its isotopes may also turn out to be mixtures of entities with different properties; and so on indefinitely. In short, Augustus de Morgan's saying, that

Great fleas have little fleas upon their backs to bite 'em,
And little fleas have lesser fleas, and so *ad infinitum*,[46]

may be as true of properties as of particulars. And if it is, then conjunctive properties will be the only properties there are.

[44] *Universals and Scientific Realism*, vol. II, ch. 15.1.
[45] p. 32.
[46] Augustus De Morgan, *A Budget of Paradoxes*, ed. Sophia Elizabeth De Morgan (London: Longmans, Green, and Co., 1872), p. 377.

However, this conclusion is not entailed by the mere possibility that nature is infinitely complex in this way. All that possibility shows is that there may be no limit to the number or complexity of the laws of nature, nor therefore to how many properties the Ramsey sentence Σ must quantify over. But given the infinitely many simple volumes, masses, temperatures, etc., over which Σ must quantify anyway, it can hardly have to quantify over conjunctions of them to accommodate a merely possible complexity that no one has shown to be actual.

Armstrong's other argument for conjunctive properties is that a particular a's being both F and G may give it causal powers that neither property alone would give it.[47] That is true: how cold a cold wind feels, for example, depends on its speed as well as its temperature. But all this shows is that some laws of nature have conjunctive antecedents, just as some have disjunctive or negative ones. Take the gas laws that make a balloon's volume V depend on its pressure P and its temperature T. To infer that V must depend also (or instead) on the conjunctive property $P \wedge T$, is like inferring that *The Mikado* must have been written not only (or not even) by Gilbert and Sullivan, but by their mereological sum, the two-headed conjunctive particular G+S. Both inferences seem to me as absurd as they are optional.

In short, I see no reason to accept any of the alleged counter-examples to Ramsey's test. But I do need to say more about the properties that pass it, as I do about the particulars that pass Quine's test. Quine's test rules out complex particulars, of course, just as Ramsey's rules out complex properties, and for the same reason: Quine's first-order quantifiers need not range over them. Yet many philosophers still believe in mereological sums, not just of Gilbert and Sullivan, but of *all* particulars.[48] I too of course believe that many things are parts of other things, as our hands are of our bodies, leaves are of plants, wheels are of cars, and atoms are of molecules. But that does not make people, plants, cars, and molecules conjunctive particulars, i.e. mereological sums of their parts, and they are not. They, like most if not all things with parts, will still pass Quine's test because, as not all truths about them are entailed by truths about their parts, our first-order quantifiers will still have to range over them. But then, since these wholes are –

---

[47]   *Universals and Scientific Realism*, vol. II, p. 35.
[48]   Lewis, *On the Plurality of Worlds*, p. 69.

literally – 'more than the [mereological] sums of their parts', their existence gives us no reason to believe that there *are* any such sums, let alone sums of Gilbert and Sullivan or of any other pairs of particulars that are not both parts of some third thing. The mereological composition of particulars is a myth.

And so it is of properties. Take the claim that temperature is, i.e. is identical to, mean kinetic energy. This entails that all truths about temperatures are entailed by truths about the kinetic energies of (e.g.) gas particles. If that was so, then temperatures would fail Ramsey's test, because the Ramsey sentence Σ of all laws would not need to quantify over them as well as over kinetic energies. But it is not so, for at least three reasons. First, it implies that all particles at rest are at absolute zero, and that speeding one of them up automatically heats it up, which is absurd. Second, isotropic radiation need not contain particles with kinetic energies in order to have a temperature, which it does. And third, in statistical mechanics the kinetic energies of gas particles do not determine a gas's temperature T: they merely give T a high chance of lying in a narrow range.

It follows that the Ramsey sentence of all laws, including those of thermodynamics, does need to quantify over temperatures, as well as over the kinetic energies of things and the frequencies of radiation. So temperatures do pass Ramsey's test, which for present purposes makes them 'simple' properties, despite the causal dependence of a gas's temperatures on the kinetic energies of its particles – just as our bodies are simple particulars despite their causal dependence on their parts. In neither case does the causal dependence of a whole on its parts reduce the whole to the mereological sum of those parts. The mereological composition of natural properties is as mythical as that of natural particulars.

7. Lewis's Natural Joints

This brings me, finally, to Lewis's theory of properties.[49] His theory differs from mine partly in terminology since, as I noted in §2, he calls any set of possible particulars a property, not just those whose members resemble each other. Those whose members resemble each other perfectly Lewis calls 'perfectly natural'. The

[49]   *On the Plurality of Worlds*, ch. 1.5.

naturalness of his other properties he measures by how simply they can be defined in terms of perfectly natural ones.[50]

Because all Lewis's properties are sets of possible particulars, and a set's identity is fixed by its members, all his possible worlds inevitably contain the same abundant properties. What is not inevitable is Lewis's further claim that all his worlds contain the same *sparse* properties, i.e. the same subset of his abundant properties whose members resemble each other. This is why Lewis calls these properties 'sparse': calling them 'natural' he says

> suggests to some people that it is supposed to be *nature* that distinguishes natural properties from the rest; and therefore that the distinction is a contingent matter, so that a property might be natural at one world but not at another. I do not mean to suggest any such thing. A property is natural or unnatural *simpliciter*, not relative to one or another world.[51]

But if, as I've argued, the properties that 'ground the objective resemblances and the causal powers of things' depend on contingent laws of nature, they are bound to vary from world to world. If natural properties are those over which the Ramsey sentence Σ of all laws has to quantify, there will *be* no temperatures in a world devoid of thermal phenomena and hence of laws governing them. This will be so even if properties are sets of exactly resembling possible particulars or tropes: for then what properties there are will still depend on the laws that determine which particulars or tropes *do* resemble each other exactly. If there were no laws of thermodynamics, the resemblance that makes a set of possible tropes or particulars be the property of being 100°C – or any other temperature – would not exist.

(None of this, by the way, makes properties entail the laws they occur in, as Sydney Shoemaker and Stephen Mumford claim.[52] For example, in Newtonian worlds, where gravity is a force in a flat spacetime, the inertial masses of things, defined by Newton's laws of motion, are independent of their velocities, which in our world they are not. Yet our world's masses, e.g. 100 gm, can still be the

---

[50]   p. 67.
[51]   fn. 44.
[52]   Shoemaker, 'Causality and Properties' [1980], in *Properties*, §9; Mumford, *Laws in Nature* (London: Routledge, 2004).

same as – or be counterparts of – the properties that link forces and accelerations in Newtonian worlds.)

My Ramsey-test theory differs from Lewis's in another way too, even if, as I do, we follow Jonathan Schaffer and take Lewis's perfectly natural properties to be those that occur in *any* law of nature, not just those of microphysics.[53] For, as we have seen, Lewis also admits more or less natural complexes of his perfectly natural properties and Ramsey's test does not. But we need no such complexes to credit nature with complex joints, as our chlorine example shows. For all the laws of chlorine chemistry need, to explain how chlorine samples resemble each other, and differ from samples of other elements, are disjunctive antecedents whose disjuncts are the simple properties of being ^{35}Cl and being ^{37}Cl. That disjunction need not correspond to a single disjunctive property, ^{35}Cl $\vee$ ^{37}Cl, of being stable chlorine, which, as we saw in §6, no one who believes in language-independent properties will believe in.

In short, Lewis's less-than-perfectly-natural properties are as superfluous as less-than-perfectly-natural particulars, like the disjunction, conjunction and negations of Gilbert and Sullivan. The naturalness of natural properties need no more come by degrees than that of the particulars whose properties they are.

---

[53] 'Two Conceptions of Sparse Properties', *Pacific Philosophical Quarterly* 85 (2004), pp. 92–102.

3

BOUNDARIES IN REALITY

Tuomas E. Tahko

Abstract
This chapter defends the idea that there must be some joints in
reality, some correct way to classify or categorize it. This may seem
obvious, but we will see that there are at least three conventionalist
arguments against this idea, as well as philosophers who have
found them convincing. The thrust of these arguments is that the
manner in which we structure, divide or carve up the world is not
grounded in any natural, genuine boundaries in the world. Ultimately they are supposed to pose a serious threat to realism. The
first argument that will be examined concerns the claim that there
are no natural boundaries in reality, the second one focuses on the
basis of our classificatory schemes, which the conventionalist claims
to be merely psychological, and the third considers the significance
of our particular features in carving up the world, such as physical
size and perceptual capabilities. The aim of this chapter is to
demonstrate that none of these objections succeed in undermin-
ing the existence of genuine joints in reality.

1. Introduction

Traditionally, realism attempts to uphold the classifications that
we observe in everyday life: apples, cats, mountains and stars are
all objects with natural boundaries – they reflect genuine joints
in reality. Such joints in reality are supposed to act as the basis of
our efforts to classify reality, and common sense suggests that most
of these attempts are successful. It is not easy to state the exact
identity-conditions of any of the mentioned things though. Mountains do not have a determinate boundary at ground level, and a
closer look will reveal that there is even vagueness concerning
Tibbles the cat and her hair.[1] However, the problem that we will
focus on is not the problem of vagueness. Rather, it is the extreme
conventionalist thesis concerning the mind-independence of
the identity-conditions of objects and kinds that a realist would

---

[1] See for instance Michael Tye, 'Vague Objects', *Mind* 99 (1990), pp. 535–57.

Classifying Reality, First Edition. Edited by David S. Oderberg. Copyright © 2013 The Authors. Book
compilation © 2013 Blackwell Publishing Ltd.

consider to 'carve nature at the joints'. The conventionalist thesis is that there are no such mind-independent identity-conditions and that all our efforts to determine natural boundaries are subjective. Extreme conventionalism may seem like an implausible view, but it has its roots in the influential work of Hilary Putnam and Michael Dummett. More recently, Achille Varzi has put forward a novel conventionalist account, focusing especially on boundaries.[2] More modest versions of conventionalism, i.e. views which take *some* boundaries to be mind-dependent, are fairly common. For instance, John Dupré's species pluralism could be considered a form of modest conventionalism, as it takes 'species' to consist of a variety of different ways to categorize biological organisms.[3] It should be noted though that modest conventionalism is not incompatible with realism. What *is* incompatible with realism is the idea that *all* objects and kinds lack mind-independent natural boundaries, and it is entirely a matter of convention as to how we decide to categorize reality – this is what Varzi's arguments suggest. Note that the problem at hand concerns both individual objects and kinds, but we will focus mainly on individual objects.

Artificial boundaries are quite familiar to us and we seem to have no trouble in admitting that they are indeed artificial while acknowledging their usefulness – borders of countries are one obvious example. We may also express the artificial/natural boundary distinction in terms of *fiat* and *bona fide* boundaries, or *de dicto* and *de re* boundaries, following Smith and Varzi.[4] It is important to recognize here that the *fiat/bona fide* distinction applies equally to the physical boundaries of objects and to the objects themselves: the physical boundary of an apple is, on the face of it, a *bona fide* boundary, and the individual apple is a *bona fide* entity.[5] However, this is exactly what the extreme conventionalist questions: when we look at the apple closely enough, it is

---

[2]   Achille C. Varzi, 'Boundaries, Continuity, and Contact', *Noûs* 31:1 (1997), pp. 26–58; Achille C. Varzi, 'Boundaries, Conventions, and Realism', in J. K. Campbell, M. O'Rourke, and M. H. Slater (Eds.), *Carving Nature at Its Joints: Natural Kinds in Metaphysics and Science* (Cambridge, MA: MIT Press, 2011), pp. 129–53.
[3]   John Dupré, *The Disorder of Things: Metaphysical Foundations of the Disunity of Science* (Cambridge, MA: Harvard University Press, 1993); John Dupré, *Humans and Other Animals* (Oxford: Oxford University Press, 2002).
[4]   Barry Smith and Achille C. Varzi, 'Fiat and Bona Fide Boundaries', *Philosophy and Phenomenological Research* 60: 2 (2000), pp. 401–20.
[5]   Smith and Varzi, 'Fiat and Bona Fide Boundaries', p. 402.

clear that, far from the smooth boundary that it appears to have, we are in fact dealing with a very loose arrangement of molecules, and further, with a swarm of subatomic particles. Familiar topological problems highlight the problem at hand: when we cut the apple in half, which half of the apple is 'open' and which one is 'closed'?[6] Moreover, problems concerning composition are all grist to the conventionalist's mill: when Tibbles the cat eats some fish, at what point does the fish become a part of Tibbles? Which criteria we apply, the extreme conventionalist will argue, is ultimately a matter of *fiat*; Tibbles may continue to exist, but its identity-conditions are not mind-independent.[7]

Here is how Varzi sees the situation:

> If all boundaries were the product of some cognitive or social *fiat*, if the lines along which we "splinter" the world depended entirely on our *cognitive* joints and on the categories that we employ in drawing up our maps, then our knowledge of the world would amount to neither more nor less than knowledge of those maps. The thesis according to which all boundaries – hence all entities – are of the *fiat* sort would take us straight to the brink of precipice, to that extreme form of conventionalism according to which "there are no facts, just interpretations". On the other hand, to posit the existence of genuine, *bona fide* boundaries – to think that the world comes pre-organized into natural objects and properties – reflects a form of naïve realism that does not seem to stand close scrutiny.[8]

The dilemma that Varzi puts forward here is the primary concern of this article. Do we have to choose between extreme conventionalism and naïve realism when it comes to the classification of reality? If we go with extreme conventionalism, we end up with a view which is remarkably close to the Dummettian 'amorphous lump' view of reality (even if Dummett was not committed to this view himself).[9] The (extreme) Conventionalist Thesis can be summarised as follows:

---

[6]   The open/closed distinction is a distinction between entities that do not and entities that do have their boundaries among their constituent parts. See Smith and Varzi, 'Fiat and Bona Fide Boundaries', pp. 406–8 for discussion on the open/closed issue.

[7]   Cf. Varzi, 'Boundaries, Conventions, and Realism', p. 140.

[8]   Varzi, 'Boundaries, Conventions, and Realism', p. 142.

[9]   E.g. Michael Dummett, *Frege. Philosophy of Language*, 2nd edn. (Cambridge, MA: Harvard University Press, 1981), p. 577.

(*The Coventionalist Thesis*) The world is 'dough' and we can cut it in a number of ways. All of these ways to cut are neutral in terms of the structure of reality; we can choose any classificatory scheme we please. How we choose to cut the dough depends on our psychological biases.

In what follows I will offer a realist response to the Conventionalist Thesis. There are three major points that are all crucial to the conventionalist stance. All of these are familiar from more modest versions of conventionalism, but Varzi combines them to produce the extreme conventionalist stance that we saw above.

Firstly, I will consider whether there in fact are any natural, *bona fide* boundaries and suggest that fundamental particles are the best candidate. Secondly, I will attempt to settle why we classify things in the way we do and what our psychological biases concerning our classificatory schemes are grounded in. Thirdly, I will examine the possibility of alternative, alien classificatory schemes and consider whether the manner in which we classify things is unique to us, or at least to beings of roughly our size and with similar perceptual devices and rational capabilities. Finally, the results of the discussion will be evaluated.

2. Are There Any Natural Boundaries?

The most obvious way to challenge the Conventionalist Thesis is to look for natural, *bona fide* entities with mind-independent boundaries. Even a single example would do: it would give us a fixed point that would help in defining other boundaries and hence serve as a basis for the classification of reality. Where might we start looking for natural boundaries given the problems even with biological species? It would maybe be best to look at smaller entities, atoms, perhaps. However, the Conventionalist Thesis applies to physics as well. For instance, different isotopes of the same element could arguably also be classified as different elements.[10] As Varzi suggests, the problem is that there are too many

---

[10] For discussion, see Robin F. Hendry, 'Elements, Compounds, and Other Chemical Kinds', *Philosophy of Science* 73 (2006), pp. 864–75.

differences in the world rather than too few, and to choose one over the others is to draw a *fiat* line.[11] We do not need to stop here though, for there are of course subatomic particles as well. Indeed, quarks and leptons, supposed fundamental particles, might be the best candidates for *bona fide* entities with well-defined boundaries. Admittedly, the concepts that we use to define these particles are perhaps subject to human contingencies as well. There might be limits to the accuracy of our measurements concerning some of the crucial variables, such as charge, that we use to determine the natural boundaries of fundamental particles. Still, it would surely be too strict a requirement to insist that we must be able to *state* the exact natural boundaries of, say, electrons. It is clear that we can determine these boundaries with an incredibly high accuracy. So, even though there may be epistemic constraints in effect here, this does not entail that the boundaries of electrons, for instance, are *fiat* boundaries.

What kind of evidence could we have to the effect that fundamental particles are *bona fide* entities?[12] I think that there is an abundance of such evidence: I contend that macroscopic objects would not be possible if *bona fide* entities did not exist. Hence, the very existence of macroscopic objects speaks in favour of *bona fide* entities. Note that this has nothing to do with whether macroscopic objects themselves are *bona fide* entities; the argument concerns the physical possibility of macroscopic objects. Here is an outline of the argument:

1. There are macroscopic objects.
2. Certain things are physically necessary for the forming of macroscopic objects, e.g. the laws that govern molecular binding.
3. The relevant laws of physics require that fundamental particles have *exact* properties, such as electric charge.
4. Fundamental particles possess these properties by physical necessity.
5. *Fiat* entities could not have these necessary properties.
6. Since there are macroscopic objects, there must be *bona fide* entities. (From 1-5.)

---

[11] Varzi, 'Boundaries, Conventions, and Realism', p. 142. See also C. Z. Elgin, 'Unnatural Science', *Journal of Philosophy* 92: 2 (1995), 289–302.

[12] The word 'particle' should be considered a place-holder for whatever our best science suggests, e.g. 'particle-like behaviour of the wavefunction'.

I take it that even the extreme conventionalist will accept the first premise, so I will proceed to analyse the other premises.

2. Certain things are physically necessary for the forming of macroscopic objects, e.g. the laws that govern molecular binding.

In the light of what we know about the forming of macroscopic objects, certain things are physically necessary: molecules must be able to form bonds, atoms must be able to form molecules, and subatomic particles must be able to form atoms. In virtue of what are these things possible? Well, physics tells us that the binding of molecules and atoms is dependent on the electron configuration of individual atoms. The electron configuration depends on the energy levels of specific electrons and is moderated by the Pauli Exclusion Principle.[13] Similarly, the manner in which subatomic particles form atoms is dependent on the individual charges of subatomic particles – the negative charges of the electrons and the positive charges of the protons. Each proton consists of three quarks which make up the total charge of the proton. These are some rudimentary constraints for the forming of macroscopic objects. The physical necessity of these constraints should be evident, although their *metaphysical* necessity is left open.

3. The relevant laws of physics require that fundamental particles have *exact* properties, such as electric charge.

We know that the total charge of stable atoms has to be zero. Unstable atoms undergo radioactive decay and are poor candidates for the sort of binding behaviour required for the forming of macroscopic objects. The picture gets more complicated when details about the underlying fundamental forces are introduced: for instance, the nucleus holds together in virtue of the strong force, which overpowers the repulsive forces between the positively charged quarks. In any case, it is obvious that the forming of macroscopic objects is a delicate matter and would not be possible if subatomic particles were arranged in an arbitrary fashion. Even if we are unable to accurately state the charges of the subatomic

[13]   The Pauli Exclusion Principle states that no two identical fermions can have the same quantum number at the same time.

particles that constitute an atom, we do know that their sum has to be zero, otherwise the atom could not be stable. The upshot of this is that there must be some things, namely electrons and quarks, which possess an exact charge.

4. Fundamental particles possess these properties by physical necessity.

It is already apparent that the forming of any kind of macroscopic objects requires a considerable amount of orderliness on the microphysical level. The laws that govern the forming of atoms and molecules would not work if there were no physical *constants*, such as the charge of electrons. Electrons are ordered into shells and the order of filling of electron energy states is governed by energy and the Pauli Exclusion Principle. Any study of electron configuration will refer to the fact that it is *impossible* for two electrons to occupy the same quantum state, as stated by the Pauli Exclusion Principle.

Everything that we observe in the natural world is dependent on electron configuration, and the ordering of electrons into shells would not be possible if electrons did not have physically necessary properties: exact mass, exact charge, and intrinsic properties such as spin and angular momentum. Furthermore, the charge of an electron, $-1.6021892 \times 10^{-19}$ coulombs, is a fundamental physical constant: the charges of all other freely existing subatomic particles that have a charge are either equal to or an integer multiple of it. Accordingly, it is a feature of the physics of the actual world that electrons have their charge by physical necessity. It may be that this is not *metaphysically* necessary – perhaps the laws of physics are not metaphysically necessary and there are possible worlds with alternative laws of physics – but all that is needed for the argument at hand is *physical* necessity. But how does it follow from this that there must be *bona fide* entities? For this we need the final premise:

5. *Fiat* entities could not have these necessary properties.

Clearly, *fiat* entities as well can possess exact properties. Consider the city of London: it has a number of exact properties at any given time, such as the number of underground stations and an annual budget. There is, however, a difference between the exact properties that the city of London or other *fiat* entities may have and the exact properties that, for instance, electrons seem to have. The latter are *necessary*, whereas *fiat* entities can only possess contingent or merely *derivative* necessary properties. Consider the different zones in the London Underground: there can be as many or as few zones as the underground authorities decide and they may be the basis of all sorts of things, such as ticket pricing. The zone division is nevertheless exact: there is no ambiguity about whether a given station is in one zone or another. At the same time, it is an entirely contingent property of the underground system that it has any zones at all. We might call it a *fiat* property: although the zoning is exact at any given time, it has no fixed requirements. It can change from time to time and we could even have decided not to introduce it at all. But we could not do anything of the sort, say, in the case of the charge of electrons, because if the charge were different then the microphysical orderliness required for the existence of macroscopic objects would collapse. That is, the exact actual charge of electrons is *necessary* for the emergence of macroscopic objects, whereas the zoning of the London Underground is thoroughly contingent.

It could be objected here that, for instance, the *fiat* entity that consists of two electrons in my left hand surely has certain necessary properties, e.g. the sum of the charges of these electrons. However, this will hardly undermine the argument, for the necessity involved here is based on the necessary properties of the individual electrons. Hence, the *fiat* entity will not have necessary properties in its own right – the necessity will have to 'piggyback' on the necessary properties of some *bona fide* entity or other. In other words, the existence of derivative necessary properties like the one described above is dependent on the existence of some primary necessary property. A closer inspection of derivative necessary properties will always reveal a primary necessary property of a *bona fide* entity – we might call it a *bona fide* property. Indeed, *bona fide* properties might be the best indicator of *bona fide* entities.

6. Since there are macroscopic objects, there must be *bona fide* entities. (From 1-5.)

We have now arrived at the conclusion of the argument: because there are macroscopic objects, there have to be *bona fide* entities that instantiate the exact, physically necessary *bona fide* properties that are needed for this macrophysical structure.

Accordingly, the very existence of macroscopic objects speaks highly in favour of the existence of *bona fide* entities.

The argument has a number of interesting ramifications. Firstly, we can use it in two ways: as a general argument for the existence of *bona fide* entities, or as a more specific argument towards the conclusion that electrons and other fundamental particles are in fact such *bona fide* entities. It could perhaps be extended into an argument for some sort of microstructural essentialism as well, but I will not pursue that line here. I only wish to establish the first point, and I think that the case for it is fairly strong. We must have some entities which uphold the intricate structure required for the forming of macroscopic objects. To do this, these entities must be able to interact in a highly complex and stable manner. This interaction is possible only in virtue of a certain set of *bona fide* properties that these entities possess. *Fiat* entities do not seem to be capable of instantiating properties of the required type – they can only have *fiat* boundaries and properties.

I am not aware of any (extreme) conventionalist discussions of fundamental particles, which is rather surprising given that they are surely the best candidates for *bona fide* entities. Furthermore, even if our current physical theory about fundamental particles is mistaken, the point that was made above would still hold. This is the case even if the particles that we think are fundamental do after all have internal structure, or if they are better understood without using 'particle-talk' at all. Whatever the fundamental constituents of reality are, they must be such that they are able to form stable atoms. More generally, subatomic particles are subject to a well-defined set of fundamental forces and their interaction is based on these forces. For this interaction to result in stable macrophysical objects, it must regularly end up in bonding behaviour. As we have seen, such bonding behaviour requires *bona fide* properties and hence *bona fide* entities with *bona fide* boundaries. This is true regardless of whether we can actually state the identity-conditions of these entities – this is merely an epistemic concern.

The most important ramification of this account is perhaps that it effectively undermines the Dummettian view of reality as an amorphous lump. One cannot accept both the Dummettian picture and the idea that fundamental particles are *bona fide* entities. Perhaps the extreme conventionalist could argue that the existence of electrons or other fundamental particles as *bona fide* entities is not required. Rather, the amorphous lump must contain local variations in such a way that the required *bona fide* properties – e.g. negative and positive charges – are present in certain regions of the amorphous lump.[14] However, if the conventionalist concedes this much, then the amorphous lump picture is already undermined: surely a lump with fixed regional variations is anything but amorphous. If the extreme conventionalist thesis suggests that all our efforts to structure reality are based on *Gestalt* factors, then fixed local variations in the amorphous lump are also ruled out. Admittedly, this line would enable the conventionalist to deny the existence of electrons as *bona fide* entities, but it does entail the existence of *bona fide* properties.

There may in fact be *some* support for this type of an approach in current physics. For instance, the GRW interpretation of quantum mechanics suggests that what we have been calling particles may be nothing else than aspects of the behaviour of the wave function.[15] However, as Peter J. Lewis puts it: 'If the GRW theory is true, then particles and elephants are both instantiated by waves, but this provides no more reason to deny the existence of particles than to deny the existence of elephants.'[16] The details are obviously more complicated than this. What is clear is that whatever the fundamental structure of the world is, it contains features which enable the existence of macroscopic objects. Accordingly, the core thesis of extreme conventionalism is already refuted: there is structure in reality and it is according to the *de re* features of reality – be it particles or waves – that we carve it up. Indeed, Varzi claims that 'The conventionalist stance simply entails that which of them [the individuals that we may postulate] come to play a role in our life is up to us.'[17] But it seems to me that it is not: we could try to ignore the structure present in the microphysical, but this would render our physical theories quite unable to do the job they were designed to do, namely, they would fail to be predictive. One central aspect

---

[14]   There are elements for a suggestion of this type in John O'Leary-Hawthorne and Andrew Cortens, 'Towards Ontological Nihilism', *Philosophical Studies* 79: 2 (1995), pp. 143–65; Terry Horgan and Matjaž Potrč, *Austere Realism: Contextual Semantics Meets Minimal Ontology* (Cambridge, MA: MIT Press, 2008); and Jonathan Schaffer, 'Monism: the Priority of the Whole', *Philosophical Review* 119: 1 (2010), pp. 31–76. See also Donnchadh O'Conaill and Tuomas E. Tahko, 'On the Common Sense Argument for Monism', in Philip Goff (Ed.), *Spinoza on Monism* (New York: Palgrave Macmillan, 2011), where Schaffer's view is discussed in detail.

[15]   The Ghirardi-Rimini-Weber (GRW) theory is one version of a 'collapse' theory of quantum mechanics.

[16]   Peter J. Lewis, 'GRW: A Case Study in Quantum Ontology', *Philosophy Compass* $^1/_2$ (2006), pp. 228–229.

[17]   Varzi, 'Boundaries, Conventions, and Realism', p. 148.

of our physical theories is to predict bonding behaviour, such as the bonding of subatomic particles into stable atoms. Since this bonding behaviour is governed by *de re* features of reality, ignoring these features would produce failing predictions.

3. Why Do We Classify Things in the Way We Do?

We already have a fairly good case against extreme conventionalism, as it appears that fundamental particles are very likely candidates for *bona fide* entities. Now we turn to another serious claim, namely that our classificatory schemes are grounded in our psychological biases, *Gestalt* factors that do not represent the structure of reality in any way:

> Consider the debate on unrestricted composition. There is no question that we feel more at ease with certain mereological composites than with others. We feel at ease, for instance, with regard to such things as the fusion of Tibbles's parts (whatever they are), or even a platypus's parts; but when it comes to such unlovely and gerrymandered mixtures as [Lewisian] trout-turkeys, consisting of the front half of a trout and the back half of a turkey, we feel uncomfortable. Such feelings may exhibit surprising regularities across contexts and cultures. Yet, arguably they rest on psychological biases and *Gestalt* factors that needn't have any bearing on how the world is actually structured.[18]

Is there any connection between how the world is structured and our evaluation of things such as trout-turkeys? Varzi argues that there might not be, as even though we initially feel uncomfortable about strange hybrids, we have nevertheless welcomed a variety of genetically manipulated plant-hybrids, such as orange-mandarins. Indeed, our intuitions and feelings of discomfort should not be relied on if we hope to determine the actual structure of reality; it is true that we are biased in our evaluations. However, psychological biases like these have little to do with scientific practice – the very existence of genetically manipulated

---

[18] Varzi, 'Boundaries, Conventions, and Realism', pp. 144–5.

hybrids is proof enough. The actual structure of reality quite clearly *does* have a bearing on our scientific practices though. The case of the trout-turkey might not seem to be directly relevant here. After all, trout-turkeys are not supposed to be results of genetic manipulation. Rather, they are just mereological sums consisting of two disconnected parts, the front half of some trout and the back half of some turkey. How do we evaluate the case of the trout-turkey in this context, then? The answer depends on our take on unrestricted mereological composition. Examples like trout-turkeys and the sum of one's nose and the Eiffel tower could certainly be seen as a *reductio* of unrestricted mereological composition, but we do not need to pursue that line of thought here. In any case, there may be good reasons for our initial, hostile reaction towards such entities: perhaps in these cases composition does *not* occur, there are no such entities.[19] To settle the issue, a thorough discussion of unrestricted mereological composition would be needed, but this is not the place for it. It might be more interesting to consider an example that is neutral in regard to questions of mereology: consider the possibility of a genetically manipulated trout-turkey hybrid.

When we consider what sort of entities could exist, we do not decide this in terms of which entities we feel comfortable with, but rather in terms of which entities are possible. How do we decide which entities *are* possible, leaving unrestricted mereological composition aside? Well, by examining the relevant sub-categories of possibility. In the case of trout-turkeys we would be interested in the *biological* possibility of these creatures, namely whether there could be a DNA sequence that produces trout-turkeys. This is of course (at least partly if not entirely) a matter for biological research. However, the space of possible organisms is also restricted by *physical* possibility, in other words we can rule out creatures that are not physically viable given the actual laws of physics. Some insects above a certain size, for instance, would be ruled out, because their respiratory system would not be able to function in this super-sized form – a trout-turkey would no doubt encounter similar problems!

[19] For more discussion on unrestricted composition, see Tuomas E. Tahko, 'Against the Vagueness Argument', *Philosophia* 37: 2 (2009), pp. 335–40. There I argue that the vagueness argument against restricted composition fails and that we have some good reasons to prefer restricted composition.

We are now faced with a question: do we have any reason to believe that the analysis of possible kinds of hybrids is based on *Gestalt* factors rather than the actual structure of reality? Admittedly, this analysis is fallible. Something that we believed to be biologically or physically impossible could turn out to be possible after all. This might even be due to *Gestalt* factors. But to claim that there is *no* structure on which our analysis is based is like claiming that a monkey could have written *The Brothers Karamazov*. If you put the monkey in front of a keyboard and it randomly beats the keyboard, it is possible to produce the book in question, but it is not very likely. Similarly, it seems that our classificatory schemes must correspond to *something*, as otherwise they would just be gibberish. How could we possibly come up with such a sophisticated structure by coincidence?[20] More importantly, our current best scientific classification scheme has enormous predictive power: we can predict a huge range of natural phenomena from chemical reactions to the movement of heavenly bodies. This predictive power must be based on something and the obvious explanation is that our classificatory schemes roughly correspond with the structure of reality. Consider an example: Mendeleev's periodic table.

Mendeleev arranged elements into a table by their atomic mass and their chemical properties, which enabled him to predict the existence of a number of yet undiscovered elements as well as the chemical properties of these elements. To start with, Mendeleev had some established empirical information about certain elements, namely their atomic masses and chemical properties. It was a natural thing to do to examine the relationships between the elements. Indeed, other similar attempts were being made around the same time as Mendeleev published his periodic table. What is interesting to us is how effective this system was in terms of making predictions about future empirical observations, namely undiscovered elements. So, the periodic table can be seen as a description of what is possible given certain building blocks. These building blocks are of course our knowledge about the atomic masses and the chemical properties of certain elements.

The modal basis of Mendeleev's work consisted of the different possible states of affairs that could explain empirical observa-

---

[20] Compare this with the 'no miracles' argument, e.g. Hilary Putnam, *Mathematics, Matter and Method* (Cambridge: Cambridge University Press, 1975).

tions.[21] The likeliest explanation for the success of Mendeleev's classificatory scheme would appear to be that it is the *correct* scheme, correct in the sense that it corresponds with the structure of reality. This does not mean that we could not reach similar results with a very different classificatory scheme, but there are certain pragmatic reasons to prefer Mendeleev's scheme, including theoretical virtues such as simplicity. However, any scheme that differs from Mendeleev's so radically that it loses predictive power, never mind theoretical virtues, will simply be an incorrect way to characterize natural phenomena.

So, why do we classify things in the way we do? Certainly, psychological biases play a role here, but only a very modest one: we are quick to abandon them if they lack predictive power. If someone were to create a trout-turkey – let us assume that it is possible – we would soon acknowledge it, regardless of how uneasy we might feel about it. Consequently, our classificatory schemes, although always subject to revision, are fundamentally based on the actual structure of reality. It may be that we are unable to ever accurately state what that structure is, but it is nevertheless the basis of our classificatory efforts. It also seems that we are getting better at classifying things all the time, judging by the increasing predictive accuracy of our classificatory schemes.

Presumably, the conventionalist will deny the inference at hand: from the predictive power of our classificatory schemes to their approximate correspondence with reality as it is in itself. The conventionalist will no doubt acknowledge that it would be absurd to abandon the theories that offer best predictive power, but it could still be insisted that this does not mean that our best theories even roughly correspond with reality. Such a Humean position is difficult to refute. The conventionalist can always fall back to the point that there are no a priori reasons to think that our classificatory systems carve reality at the joints. Perhaps this is an unfair objection, as naturally we classify things with reference to empirical feedback rather than solely on the basis of some a priori principles. But is there nothing else that we can say to convince the conventionalist?

Well, perhaps there *are* some a priori principles that guide our classificatory schemes. Fundamental (logical) principles such as

[21]   For a more extensive account on the modal basis of such tools, see Tuomas E. Tahko, 'On the Modal Content of A Posteriori Necessities', *Theoria: A Swedish Journal of Philosophy* 75: 4 (2009), pp. 344–57.

the law of non-contradiction may be the best candidates. If there are such principles, they must be principles concerning *reality* rather than merely our *thoughts about reality*. The conventionalist will perhaps insist that we have no a priori reasons to think that reality rather than our thoughts about reality conforms to the law of non-contradiction, and perhaps we indeed do not have such reasons.[22] However, the alternative is utter scepticism. If this is the route the conventionalist wishes to take, then so be it.

In defence of the realist position, we could reply that even the extreme conventionalist acts as if reality conformed to the law of non-contradiction. Even if there are no a priori reasons to think that this is the case, we can at least build a case for a high probability. As we saw, it would be miraculous if our scientific theories possessed such predictive power by sheer luck. Accordingly, the choice between extreme conventionalism and realism should be easy.

4. Is Our Classificatory System Unique?

Even if we can dismiss utter scepticism, some doubts about just how accurately our systems of classification correspond with reality may remain. After all, the manner in which we classify things surely has something to do with our particular psychological biases, which depend on our rational capabilities and physical characteristics. We are beings of a certain size, our senses are tuned in a certain way, and our brains have a certain capacity. Accordingly, it may be that beings that differ from us in regard to one or more of these features have a very different way of carving up reality.

Let us start with animals. For instance, we know that dogs can hear frequencies that we are not able to hear, and we can see things that they cannot see, namely certain colours. Presumably our rational capabilities also differ substantially from those of dogs. Naturally, there will be striking differences between how dogs perceive and classify reality and how we do. Just how striking will these differences be? Dogs are unlikely to have any grasp of

---

[22] For an extensive discussion of the interpretation of the law of non-contradiction and a defence of the idea that it is a principle concerning reality itself rather than our thoughts about reality, see Tuomas E. Tahko, 'The Law of Non-Contradiction as a Metaphysical Principle', *The Australasian Journal of Logic* 7 (2009), pp. 32–47.

atoms or natural kinds, but they do clearly have some grasp of distinctions like edible and non-edible, friendly and hostile, leader of the pack and member of the pack. In other words, there is some overlap between how dogs carve up reality and how we do, even if there are also major differences. Many of these differences are based on physical factors which cannot be overcome, but some of them could perhaps be mapped to correspond with our framework of classification. For instance, a dog would determine what is edible primarily with his sense of smell, whereas we would often have to rely on taste, but the result might still be the same. In any case, the major problem in mapping the dog framework to ours is that dogs do not possess similar rational capabilities and thus their classificatory framework will necessarily be quite rudimentary compared to ours. An open question is whether the dog framework is based on similar methods of classification, such as predictive power. But whatever the basis of their classificatory scheme, we know that dogs have the capacity for learning. Learning takes advantage of the same features of reality that our scientific theories do: regularities that can be predicted.

Perhaps a more interesting example than dogs would be beings of intellect roughly similar to ours. As there are no obvious examples on Earth, we may take some sort of aliens as an example. Let us assume that they have roughly the same brain capacity and are similarly developed compared to humans. These aliens, although their physical constitution is roughly similar to ours otherwise, have no eyesight. Instead, they use sophisticated sonar.[23] Once again, there will necessarily be major differences between our and the alien framework of classification. For one thing, colour concepts would be quite meaningless to the alien species, as their sonar would be to us. However, the important cases do not concern everyday experiences, but scientific classifications. Consider elements: could the aliens have anything similar to the periodic table of elements which is so familiar and important to us? Their means to acquire information about the elements would certainly be different from ours, given that sight plays a major role for us. But then again, things like colour concepts are completely unnecessary for stating something like 'Hydrogen is the lightest element.' If we assume that the aliens

[23] 'Martian sonar' like this has been discussed in Gregory McCulloch, 'What it is Like', *The Philosophical Quarterly* 38: 150 (1988), pp. 1–19.

have tools fit for their senses that enable them to examine atoms, then it would be strange if they did not have some grasp of what 'the lightest element' means. It does not matter in what way they come to know that there is a lightest element. Provided that the aliens are at all scientifically minded, they will want to explain the same natural phenomena that we do. They might not have anything like our periodic table of elements though. Perhaps their information about the elements would be arranged in a table according to the sound output that their sophisticated sonar microscope produces. In any case, whatever the format of their table of elements might be, it would still contain information about the relationships between different elements just as the periodic table does. We can assume this with confidence because the relationships between different elements are crucial for an understanding of chemical reactions, which is what any intelligent being would surely hope to acquire. It would be possible for the aliens as it is for us to arrange elements by their electron configuration, and it is likely that the aliens could also predict still unobserved elements with the help of their table, as Mendeleev was able to do with his.

The upshot is that superficial differences between classificatory systems are not important. These differences could, at least in principle, be mapped to correspond – translated to match each other. This is of course possible because the subject-matter of the systems is the same: the elements are the same for anyone who might wish to observe them. It is not relevant whether we would be able to perform the translation; all that matters is that there is a theoretical correspondence.

One further objection could be raised about both of the previous examples, as they deal with beings roughly the same size as us. An important limitation to the way we perceive the world is indeed our physical size. If there were beings, say, the size of atoms or the size of galaxies, they would surely have a thoroughly different point of view towards reality.

On the face of it, this is correct. Atoms and galaxies differ so radically from us in terms of size that we can barely comprehend just how small and large they are, respectively. Only some hundreds of years ago we did not even know about things like atoms and galaxies, and our system of classification did not, of course, include them. We only classified things that we could observe and understand. In this sense we indeed had a psychological bias dependent on our physical size. However, now we *do* know about atoms and galaxies, and even about entities much smaller and larger than these. We may not be able to fully grasp the scale of these things, but we can express it accurately in numerical form and in comparison to our own size. In fact, our most important classifications now arguably concern things that are either vastly smaller or larger than us.

The question is, would beings much smaller or larger than us classify things in the same way as we do? Well, naturally they would face the same initial limitations due to their size as we did, but what if they did have some means to observe the same scale that we do? It seems to me that the answer is very clear: at first any kind of intelligent beings would be most interested in things of roughly similar size to themselves. But if they had the means to observe the same scale as we do, they would certainly wish to classify things falling into that scale. It is obvious that there would be differences in all three systems of classification – ours, the atom-sized beings, and the galaxy-sized beings – but once again it should be at least theoretically possible to map these differences so that the systems would correspond. This is because each system, provided that we could observe the same scale of things, would no doubt have roughly the same number of different *kinds* of entities. Each system would perhaps be more detailed in regard to its own scale, simply because it is easier to observe things roughly of our own size, but we would of course be more than happy to amend our own system of classification to accommodate any details that we might learn from the systems of the atom-sized beings or the galaxy-sized beings.

Yet another concern related to our physical size, and perhaps also to our perception of time, is that our conception of the persistence conditions of certain objects may be very different from the conception of creatures much smaller and larger than us, or creatures much more short- or long-lived than us. For instance, we would perhaps consider a lake to be unable to survive complete evaporation of all the water it is composed of. The lake has dried, even though the water is simply undergoing its natural cycle and will eventually rain down somewhere. But for some very short-lived, microscopic beings, tiny water droplets invisible to the naked eye might be rather similar to how lakes are for us. Yet, we would hardly consider anything to have been lost if such a water droplet were to evaporate – after all, this happens all the time in the natural cycle of water. Similarly, for some extremely long-lived and large creatures lakes might be quite like the tiny water drop-lets are for us.

Perhaps there are indeed some psychological biases here which cannot be overcome, as certain objects will simply not have a similar relevance for us and for beings of a very different size or temporal persistence. However, the fact that we might not pay much attention to tiny water droplets does not mean that they are not included in our ontology in some sense. We might not count them as *bona fide* entities, and the argument at hand may be reason enough to dismiss lakes as *bona fide* entities as well. But it is certainly not enough to motivate extreme conventionalism. In any case, I take it that two object-candidates which have the same properties save for size would presumably have the same (or nearly the same) persistence conditions as well. The problem is to produce a plausible story about when composition occurs, but that is something that we cannot settle here.

Admittedly, the whole scenario is rather strange: it does not appear that intelligent beings of the size of atoms or galaxies are possible. Then again, this might just be a psychological bias due to our physical size! At any rate, we do know that there are organisms so small that we cannot observe them with the naked eye. It may also be that, say, for beings the size of atoms, it would be physically impossible to observe anything much larger than themselves. Thus, if they were intelligent, their system of classification would be bound to atom-sized things, rendering it fundamentally alien to us. Nevertheless, although size and perceptual capabilities play a central role in our classificatory schemes, they can at least to a large extent be overcome with the help of tools, such as the microscope and the telescope. So they are nothing more than a hindrance. The list of entities waiting to be classified is the same for everyone – size does not matter.

5. Realism Refuted?

Where do we stand now that we have discussed three major conventionalist lines of criticism against realism about classification? Not far from where we started. The conventionalist will need some fairly strong arguments to undermine realism, for the alternative is not particularly attractive. As Varzi admits: 'Surely the *intuitive* plausibility [of the conventionalist stance] is pretty low, and perhaps also its scientific tenability.'[24] Varzi claims that convention-

[24] Varzi, 'Boundaries, Conventions, and Realism', p. 148.

alism nevertheless has some philosophical advantages, but these would need to be demonstrated thoroughly to give conventionalism any hope of overcoming its initial implausibility. Furthermore, the arguments that we have discussed appear to be inadequate to undermine the plausibility of realism.

We have seen that our system of classification is fundamentally grounded in reality. We can state this with some confidence, as otherwise this system would hardly be so reliable. It is an open question which entities are genuine, *bona fide* entities; we need philosophical inquiry as well as science to determine this. We saw that fundamental particles, whatever they are, are likely candidates for *bona fide* entities – otherwise macroscopic objects would not be possible. Furthermore, although intelligent beings different from us might have very different systems of classification, their systems as well must share the same basis. In conclusion, realism about classification stands its ground: all major lines of criticism available to the extreme conventionalist can be addressed.

4

CONTRASTIVE EXPLANATIONS IN
EVOLUTIONARY BIOLOGY

Stephen Boulter

Abstract
Taxonomists in biology have traditionally been concerned to
delimit and classify *actual* (or previously *actual*) biological forms or
kinds. But not all useful classification schemes are of *actualised*
forms. This chapter focuses on the need to delimit and classify
non-actual forms when offering contrastive explanations in evolutionary biology. Such a classification scheme sorts *actual* and *non-
actual* forms according to their *modal* status. Such a sorting has
been offered by theoretical morphologists, but these efforts have
paid insufficient attention to the metaphysics of modality. Contemporary approaches to the metaphysics and epistemology of modality are also found wanting. The chapter ends by arguing that the
needed intellectual resources are to be found in the imaginative
use of Aristotle.

1. Introduction

It is hard to over-estimate the importance of taxonomy to our
understanding of biological phenomena. One need only appreciate the dependence of the comparative method on a reliable
taxonomy, and the centrality of this method to much of biology,
to see that an adequate delimitation and classification of biological forms is the foundation on which the more eye-catching
branches of biology are built.[1] However, the theory and practice of
delimiting and classifying actual biological forms is not the focus
of attention here. The concerns of this chapter are the much less
familiar but arguably no less important challenges facing those
wishing to sort actual and non-actual biological forms into the
various modal categories. Most pressing is the need to light upon

---

[1]   For excellent discussions of both points see Ernst Mayr's *Systematics and the Origins of
Species from the Viewpoint of a Zoologist* (Cambridge Mass.: Harvard Universwity Press, 1942)
and Paul Harvey and Mark Pagel's *The Compatative Method in Evolutionary Biology* (Oxford:
Oxford University Press, 2000).

Classifying Reality, First Edition. Edited by David S. Oderberg. Copyright © 2013 The Authors. Book
compilation © 2013 Blackwell Publishing Ltd.

a principled means of determining in the case of any given non-actual form if it is non-actual but biologically possible, or non-actual because impossible. And if a given form is impossible, we also need to be able to determine if its impossibility is due to biological, physical, metaphysical or logical factors.

It is not immediately obvious why a sorting of biological forms on modal criteria is required, so the first section of this essay is devoted to motivating this particular taxonomic project. The second section establishes that the intellectual resources necessary to carry out the required sorting are not available in contemporary approaches to modality. The final section argues that the Aristotelian approach to modality provides positive guidance on how the required sorting is to be carried out in practice.

2. The Modal Categories and Contrastive Explanations

The need to sort actual and non-actual biological forms on modal criteria stems from the fact that explanations in evolutionary biology are essentially contrastive. Very often the contrasts of interest are those obtaining between an *actual* form and a range of other suitably chosen *actual* forms. But this is not always the case. Very often a biologist will not fully understand an actual form without first comparing it to a range of non-actual forms. This is particularly so with respect to evolutionary biology's two self-imposed explanatory tasks, viz., explaining biological diversity, and explaining organismal design. In such cases the biologist is always asking why a given trait or feature obtains *rather than some other trait or feature*. Dennett offers a particularly clear expression of this point:

> 'Any acceptable explanation of the patterns we observe in the Tree of Life must be contrastive: why do we see this actual pattern rather than that one – or no pattern at all? What are the nonactualised alternatives that need to be considered, and how are they organised? To answer such questions, we need to be able to talk about what is possible in addition to what is actual.'[2]

Those interested in the metaphysics of causation will note a significant point here. Since explanations in biology are causal, it

---

[2]   *Darwin's Dangerous Idea* (London: Penguin, 1995, p. 103).

would appear that biologists are lending tacit support to a controversial but plausible claim regarding the number of roles one must posit in any causal relation. On the view adopted here the form of a causal relation is always 'c_1 rather than c_2 or c_3 or c_n causes e_1 rather than e_2, or e_3 or e_n' despite the fact that the contrasting causes and alternative effects are usually left unexpressed.[3]

Now it is the need to specify the modal character of the alternative effects in biological explanations that is the focus of attention here. To make progress on explaining why the Tree or Mosaic of Life has the shape it does, for example, the biologist needs to explain why life on Earth presents precisely *this* degree of diversity and no more. And this question arises precisely because biologists have hitherto assumed, quite plausibly, that life on Earth has *not* exhausted all the genuine biological possibilities. Indeed some go much further and insist that '[t]he actual animals that have ever lived on earth are a tiny subset of the theoretical animals that could exist.'[4] If this is so, then it is perfectly natural to wonder why just these organisms made it to actuality while the vast majority of conceivable organisms did not. As McGhee puts it, when explaining biological diversity, '[t]he ultimate goal is to understand why extant form actually exists and why non-existent form does not.'[5] But addressing this question successfully presupposes the ability to trace the boundaries between distinct modal categories. First, one must be able to distinguish between the non-actual but possible forms and the non-actual because impossible forms; second, among the impossible forms, one must be able to distinguish between the biologically, physically, metaphysically and logically impossible forms, each form of impossibility being a distinct modal category with different implications for explanation. For the explanation of why the world contains ambulatory pigs and carnivorous snakes, say, but *not* flying pigs or vegetarian snakes, depends in large part on whether flying pigs

---

[3]   The need for contrastive causes and alternative effects for determinate causal/ explanatory relations seems to be accepted even by binary causal theorists given that they must posit a field of contrasts in order to identify causes.

[4]   Richard Dawkins, *The Blind Watchmaker* (London: Longmans, 1986, p. 73). Dawkins is not alone in this regard. Theodosius Dobzhansky writes: 'The variety of these possible ways of living – ecological niches is . . . great.' *The Genetics of the Evolutionary Process* (New York: Columbia University Press, 1970, p. 27).

[5]   McGhee, G. R. *Theoretical Morphology: The Concept and its Applications* (New York: Columbia University Press, 1999, p. 2).

and vegetarian snakes are non-actual but possible organisms or simply impossibilities. The first suggests that nature has simply not got round to making flying pigs or vegetarian snakes – perhaps the necessary mutations in the pig or snake populations have yet to occur, or perhaps incipient flying pigs and vegetarians snakes have arisen but have been actively selected against in past environments. But if such organisms are simply impossibilities, then flying pigs and vegetarian snakes were never an option because such organisms cannot be made. Natural selection would then have nothing to do with such organisms failing to reach actuality. I will return to this explanatory difference shortly, but the main point for present purposes is that for the biologist to fully understand extant forms she must have a reliable grasp of the modal character of the extant forms and that of the alternative effects. Efforts in this direction are found in theoretical morphology, the aim of which is 'an understanding of biological diversity, framed in terms of the boundaries between the possible and the actual and the possible and the impossible.'[6]

Being able to trace the boundary between the non-actual but possible and the non-actual because impossible is also crucial to the other explanatory task of evolutionary biology – accounting for organismal design. The leading idea here has been to advert to the notion of adaption. And the task has been to establish in any given case whether the trait in question is an adaptation, the operating assumption being that the sheer existence of a trait does not imply adaptive significance. To establish that a trait is an adaptation one needs to show (amongst other things) that it was selected from a range of alternative values for the trait, for a trait is an adaptation, not if it is absolutely optimal, but if it is optimal vis-à-vis a range of real alternatives. Since it is usually impossible to know empirically what the variations within the population in the ancestral environment actually were (since these have long been eliminated from the population) biologists must find some other way of identifying a plausible range of alternative values for the trait. Again, to do this biologists must construct a 'morphospace' representing hypothetical yet potentially existent morphologies. The idea is that they can then

---

[6]   Hickman, C. S. "Theoretical design space: A new program for the analysis of structural diversity" in Seilacher and Chinzei, eds., *Progress in Constructional Morphology. Neues Jahrbuch fur Geologie und Palaontology, Abhandlungen*, 1990: 170.

compare this set of possibilities with reality to see which of the possible forms are common, rare or non-existent. They can then carry out a functional analysis of both existent and non-existent forms to see if the existent forms are of adaptive significance. But again the point for present purposes is that meeting the second of the self-imposed explanatory tasks presupposes that the biologist has a reliable grasp of the modal character of the alternative effects. Without such a grasp any conclusions based on comparisons of functional analyses are very likely to be unsound since one might include within the morphospace conceivable but biologically impossible values for the trait. Such a conflation of the biologically possible and impossible could result in a trait's adaptive significance being missed, say, because a conceivable though biologically impossible value for the trait performs better on a functional analysis than the actual value despite the fact that the actual value is the best of the real alternatives.

So much is clear about the contrastive nature of biological explanations, and why a reliable means of sorting actual and non-actual forms on modal criteria is required. But what is also clear, yet seldom discussed with the requisite urgency, is that as yet there is no widely accepted means of sorting forms into modal categories. Indeed one of the great controversies in contemporary biology – the dispute concerning the principal driver of evolutionary change – turns in large part upon different intuitions regarding what is biologically possible. Orthodox neo-Darwinians, and their bug-bear, Stephen J. Gould, often talk as though what is biologically possible is virtually limitless. This modal claim suits both camps well. It fits nicely with the neo-Darwinian view that natural selection is the main, and perhaps the exclusive, explanatory tool of evolutionary biology, for it is natural selection that allegedly winnows this vast expanse of genuine possibilities down to the few lucky winners that make it to actuality. And it fits Gould's intuitions that life on Earth would be very different if history, with all its contingencies, were to be re-run. But both Gould and the neo-Darwinians face a serious challenge from another school of thought, with roots in the work of D'Arcy Thompson, which maintains that the range of genuine biological possibilities is actually severely limited, and so the explanatory import of natural selection or historical contingencies is greatly diminished. In his provocatively titled *Evolution without Selection* Lima-de-Faria writes:

'Biological evolution exists for the simple reason that it could not be avoided. The proton, the neutrino and the boson contained at the dawn of the formation of the universe the properties that would make later plant and animal evolution inevitable. Moreover, but most important, this biological evolution arose as a prisoner of the rules and principles guiding the initial construction of energy and matter and as such cannot follow any lines of development except the narrow ones imposed by this initial restrictions and canalisation. Biological form and biological function are the products of the mould of form and function already present in the quarks and leptons, or in any other of the elementary particles.'[7]

On this line of thought physico-chemical constraints are accorded pride of place with natural selection and historical contingencies reduced to a marginal role. But the point for present purposes is that there is no principled way to decide between the neo-Darwinians and Gould on the one hand, and the structuralists on the other, without an adequate grasp of the modal character of both the actual and alternative effects.[8] One illustration taken from Lima-de-Faria will suffice. Why do humans smile? Neo-Darwinians will say that at some stage of hominid evolution there was selective advantage to be had from the ability to smile, and this

---

[7]   (New York: Elsevier, 1988, xx). Simon Conway Morris sides with Lima-de-Faria on this point inasmuch as he takes certain evolutionary events to be virtually inevitable. See his *The Crucible of Creation: The Burgess Shale and the Rise of Animals.* (Oxford: Oxford University Press, 1998), and *Life's Solutions: Inevitable Humans in A Lonely Universe* (Cambridge: Cambridge University Press, 2004) for a perspective very much at odds with that expressed by Gould in *Wonderful Life: The Burgess Shale and the Nature of History* (London: Vintage, 2000).

[8]   The following set of contradictory theses about biological possibility and the explanatory power of natural selection is taken from Lima-de-Faria's *Evolution without Selection* (pp. 311–329). They illustrate the lack of professional consensus on biological modalities. The first in each pair is generally upheld by neo-Darwinian orthodoxy, the second by structuralists: 1. Biological evolution results from randomness and selection/Biological evolution is totally conditioned by order found at the sub-atomic, elemental and mineral levels. 2. There are no physico-chemical constraints in gene and chromosome evolution/ The genetic apparatus was severely canalised when the gene and chromosome were formed. 3. Every type of cell, organism and trait is considered possible/Only certain types of cell organelles, of cells and of organisms were allowed to emerge. 4. Evolution has involved increased opportunities for variation/Evolution created a restriction at every new step. 5. The number of forms is unlimited due to randomness and selection/The number of forms is limited and small, due to constraints imposed by the original construction of matter. The human smile is a function considered to be a legacy of natural selection conferring 'advantage'/the human smile defies interpretation by selection because it is automatic, like pain. As such it agrees with an interpretation based on the autoevolution of function.

trait was selected from a range of alternative traits. That is, it was biologically possible for humans *not* to have the ability to smile, but this possibility was selected against. A structuralist like Lima-de-Faria rejects this explanation precisely because he maintains that the ability to smile in humans is *not* one of many alternatives but was forced by physico-chemical constraints having nothing whatsoever to do with selection.

At present there is no principled way of deciding who is right about the modal status of traits like smiling. This state of affairs places evolutionary biology in a particularly unwelcome position. For no putative explanation of a given phenomenon is warranted if it cannot eliminate relevant alternative explanations in a principled fashion. So, as things stand, evolutionary biologists appear to be committed to the following inconsistent set of individually plausible propositions:

1. One of the great merits of the neo-Darwinian synthesis is its extraordinary explanatory power. Indeed this explanatory power is one of the best reasons we have for accepting this theory as a true account of the living world.
2. Explanations in evolutionary biology are couched in terms of contrastive causes and alternative effects.
3. Contrastive explanations presuppose a reliable grasp of the modal character both of the effect and the non-actualised alternatives, but
4. There is currently no consensus on how to determine the modal character of the effect and the non-actualised alternatives.

When presented in this fashion the challenge facing evolutionary biology is obvious enough. The explanatory power of evolutionary biology must be illusory if (2), (3) and (4) are true. I do not wish to abandon evolutionary biology, nor do I think this is a serious option. But I see no way of plausibly denying (2) and (3). The only way to deal with this challenge is to rectify the state of affairs described by (4).

Of course this challenge is particularly embarrassing for biology. But there are good grounds for claiming that the real shame is philosophy's. For on a plausible view of the division of labour between the disciplines, it falls to metaphysics to delimit the possible, necessary and impossible, while it is the business of the special sciences, in this case biology, to determine empirically which of the possibilities have been actualised in the real world.[9] But metaphysics has not lived up to its part of the bargain. In the next section I will show that none of the approaches to the ontology and epistemology of modality currently popular in mainstream metaphysical circles is even remotely helpful when considered from a biological point of view.[10] Little wonder that biologists themselves have stepped into the breach. Unfortunately the most sophisticated efforts to date in theoretical morphology are inadequate since morphospaces are determined by the dictates of geometry alone, and are developed without reference to real organisms. This is clear enough from the following extended passage from McGhee:

'. . . the goal is to explore the possible range of morphological variability that nature could produce by constructing *n*-dimensional geometric hyperspaces (termed "theoretical morphospaces"), which can be produced by systematically varying the parameter values of a geometrical model of form. Such a morphospace is produced without any reference to real or existent organic form. Once constructed, the range of existent variability in form may be examined in this hypothetical morphospace, both to quantify the range of existent form and to reveal non-existent organic form. That is, to reveal morphologies that theoretically could exist (and can be produced by the computer) but that have never been produced in the process of organic evolution on planet Earth.'[11]

Unless one believes that the constraints of geometry exhaust the constraints placed on the living world, so that the *biologically* possible extends to the *geometrically* possible, current efforts in theoretical morphology cannot be accepted as satisfactory.[12]

---

[9] This account of the intellectual division of labour is developed by E.J. Lowe in *The Possibility of Metaphysics* (Oxford: Oxford University Press, 2001).
[10] The significance of this point should not be underplayed. The best warrant one can provide for a metaphysical theory is precisely its ability to resolve puzzles of the sort identified above while preserving as much of the science as possible. For an extended defence of this claim see my "The Aporetic Method and the Defence of Immodest Metaphysics" forthcoming in *Aristotle on Methodology and Metaphysics*. Feser (ed). (Houndmills: Palgrave Macmillan).
[11] McGhee, G.R. *Theoretical Morphology: The concept and its applications* (New York: Columbia University Press, 1999, p. 2).
[12] There does not appear to be any purely geometrical constraint that would rule out the existence of cat-sized insects, for example. But since insects lack lungs, there are physical

3. The Poverty of Orthodox Approaches to Modality

For reasons outlined in the previous section we are in the market for principled method of sorting actual and non-actual biological forms according to their modal character. We need to be able to do this in order to tell which of a variety of causes might legitimately be adverted to as an explanatory mechanism for any given biological form. Intuitions amongst biologists on this score differ dramatically, so I take it that a return to first principles is required.

Now it is very difficult to discern what is possible and impossible in any domain if one does not know what features of reality ground the modal facts in that domain. So I take it that we need both an ontology and epistemology of the biological modalities. Unfortunately we do not get much help on these matters when we turn to the contemporary theories of modality developed by mainstream metaphysicians. Space considerations allow only a brief overview of these approaches, but even a brief word on these matters is enough to appreciate that contemporary metaphysics is not going to come to our aid.

Let us remind ourselves of our task: To achieve the explanatory aims of evolutionary biology we need to know of any given biological trait or configuration of the Tree of Life if it is necessary or merely contingent. If necessary, we need to know if it is logically, metaphysically, physically, or biologically necessary. If contingent, we need to know if it is logically, metaphysically, physically or biologically contingent. And similarly for all non-actualised alternatives. Are these non-actualised alternatives non-actual because they are impossible? If so, is that impossibility of a logical, metaphysical, physical or biological nature? If the alternative is non-actual but possible, is that possibility of a logical, metaphysical, physical or biological nature? I am assuming that these modal categories are related but distinct, and, barring impressive evidence to the contrary, that all categories are occupied. The challenge is to sort actual and alternative effects into these categories. With this task in mind it is easy to see that most contemporary approaches to modality are of little use.

Take the ontological question first: what grounds the modal facts of interest to us? Various answers are on offer. Modal

---

constraints on how much oxygen they can absorb, limits which constrain how large their bodies can become. So a morphospace that allowed for cat-sized insects would conflate the non-actual because physically impossible with the non-actual but biologically possible.

eliminativism, for example, claims the only necessities, possibilities and impossibilities that exist are logical necessities, possibilities and impossibilities, thus doing away with most of our categories. There simply are no facts that allow for the fine grained distinctions the biologist needs to draw. Obviously such a view offers no assistance because it fails to recognise the full range of modalities the biologist takes seriously.[13]

Modal primitivism, on the other hand, acknowledges non-logical modality, but insists that all non-logical modalities are primitive, non-reducible, non-analysable features of reality, thus debarring herself from offering principled suggestions as to how to sort alternative effects according to their modal character.

Modal conventionalism, i.e., the view that all modality is grounded in our linguistic conventions, is another non-starter. Biologists will contend, quite rightly, that the extent and configuration of morphospace have nothing whatsoever to do with our linguistic conventions if only because these are very late arrivals on the biological stage, and it is simply not credible to maintain that the facts which fix the biological modalities had to await the arrival of human language before they could be born.

This leaves the various possible worlds approaches to modality so loved by contemporary metaphysicians. On these approaches what grounds the modal facts are possible worlds construed either as (a) distinct, concrete, causally isolated worlds[14], or (b) abstract objects, usually maximally consistent sets of sentences or propositions[15], or (c) fictional entities.[16] None of these models is attractive from a biological point of view. It is not clear, for one, how states of affairs in causally isolated worlds could be the ontological ground of biological states of affairs in this world. Second, *n'en déplaise à* Plato, it is far from clear how abstract objects of any kind could be the ontological ground of features of concrete entities such as biological forms. And, of course, fictional entities cannot be the ground of any real thing, so *a fortiori* cannot be the ground of biological forms.

Popular contemporary approaches to the epistemology of modality do not inspire much confidence either when considered

[13]   See my "The Medieval Origins of Conceivability Arguments", *Metaphilosophy*, Vol. 42, No. 5, 2011: 617–641, for the roots of modal eliminativism.
[14]   See David Lewis, *On the Plurality of Worlds* (Oxford: Blackwell, 1986).
[15]   See Alvin Plantinga, *The Nature of Necessity* (Oxford: Clarendon Press, 1974).
[16]   See Gideon Rosen, "Modal Fictionalism", *Mind*, 99, 1990: 327–54.

from a biological point of view. The most widely discussed approaches have sought to develop a connection between what we can *imagine* and our beliefs about modality. For example, conceivability based accounts of the epistemology of modality assert that the conceivability of a state of affairs entails the metaphysical possibility of that state of affairs, or at least counts as evidence for the metaphysical possibility of that state of affairs. An analogous relationship between inconceivability and metaphysical impossibility can also be entertained. When fleshing out just what is involved in conceiving one usually finds the role of the imagination coming to the fore. For example, Yablo argues that p is conceivable for some particular agent if that agent can *imagine* a possible world that would verify p.[17] P is inconceivable if the agent cannot *imagine* a possible world which verifies p. Imagination plays the same role in counterfactual based accounts of the epistemology of non-logical modality. Williamson, for example, maintains that metaphysical modality reduces to logically equivalent subjunctive conditionals, and the epistemology of metaphysical modality is nothing more than the epistemology of counterfactual reasoning. The idea here is that to establish that p is possible one imagines p to obtain and then one runs a mental simulation in which one imagines what else would be the case given p. If nothing contradictory arises in the simulation then p is deemed possible. If the simulation generates a contradiction then p is deemed impossible. As Williamson says, '. . . our fallible imaginative evaluation of counterfactuals has a conceivability test for possibility and an inconceivability test for impossibility . . .'[18]

Unfortunately these accounts will not to impress biologists. First, it is not clear that such methods could ever generate the fine grained distinctions we need to meet our challenge. But the main concern from a biological point of view is the undue confidence philosophers appear to have in the reliability of our powers of imagination to delimit and classify the field of non-actual but possible states of affairs. Most biologists are likely to agree that all biological organs, including the brain, have evolved under selective pressures (although, as we have seen, they need to be careful about this). Adaptive value in the ancestral environment is the primary explanation for a trait spreading in a population, and this

---

[17] Stephen Yablo, "Is Conceivability a Guide to Possibility?" *Philosophical and Phenomenological Research*, 53, 1993: 1–42.

[18] Williamson, Timothy, *The Philosophy of Philosophy* (Oxford: Blackwell, 2007, p. 163).

applies to belief formation processes as much as any other. But
there were no ecological or social factors in play in the ancestral
environment that generated selective pressures favouring the
emergence of a cognitive capacity that produces true beliefs about
all possible alternative configurations of the world, for there are
few biological costs involved in having false beliefs about such
matters. So while it is undoubtedly true that the ability to imagine
some non-actual situations was a tremendous cognitive advantage
in the ancestral environment, there is little reason to assume that
these advantages presuppose the ability to accurately imagine and
thereby identify *all* possibilities, let alone sort them into the
various categories. The upshot is that there is no good reason to
think that our powers of imagination are particularly reliable, and
it is a rationalist conceit to maintain otherwise.[19]

It would appear then that there is little to be had from current
approaches to the ontology and epistemology of modality in the
way of suggestions as to how one is to determine the modal
character of the actual and alternative effects featuring in certain
kinds of biological explanations. So let us now consider a radically
different approach to these issues stemming from a distinct philosophical tradition.

4. Aristotle on Modality

To have any hope of reaching a consensus on the sorting of
alternative effects in biological explanations according to modal
character I suggest we need an ontology and epistemology of
modality based on two key assumptions: First, that the modal facts
of a given domain are ontologically grounded in the actual features of the entities that make up that domain in this, the actual,
world. Second, our epistemology of modality should *not* place
emphasis on our powers of imagination. When applied to the
biological context a natural first suggestion is that one ought to
assume that morphospace is fixed first and foremost by features of
actual biological forms, and that one gains cognitive access to this
morphospace by investigating the empirically available features of
actual forms.

---

[19] See chapter 3 of Robert Nozick's *Invariances* (Cambridge, MA: Harvard University
Press, 2003). See also my "The 'evolutionary argument' and the Metaphilosophy of
Common Sense", *Biology and Philosophy*, Vol. 22, no. 3, 2007: 369–382 for a detailed
discussion of this line of thought.

Now the interest of Aristotle in this context is that he develops an approach to the ontology and epistemology of modality that meets our requirements very nicely. Thus there is a chance, or so I contend, of rectifying the situation outlined in (4) if we avail ourselves imaginatively of the metaphysics of Aristotle.[20]

Three key Aristotelian theses regarding modality are crucial to what follows. The first is that we have to recognise two distinct kinds of possibility. The first is absolute possibility. In Aristotelian terminology, a *proposition* is absolutely possible if the predicate term is not incompatible with the subject term. This kind of possibility has everything to do with the coherence of our thoughts. But there is a second kind of possibility, and that is possibility relative to some *power*. In this sense something is possible if some power can bring it about. It is this kind of possibility that falls within the purview of the natural sciences, and it is this sense of possibility that is of interest to us. The second key thesis is that the possibilities that exist in relation to some power are ontologically grounded in essences of the actually existing objects which have the relevant powers.[21] The leading idea here is that it is an entity's nature which sets the boundaries of possibility for it because a nature is ultimately a set of powers and liabilities. A corollary of this is that there is no possibility in a domain that is not ontologically grounded in some actuality of that domain. In the biological case, all real biological possibilities are ontologically grounded in the essences of actual forms. The third key claim is that the epistemology of relative possibility reduces to the epistemology of essences. This in turn is largely a matter of determining the causal powers and liabilities of a given object, an enterprise well within the bounds of ordinary scientific investigation.

This approach to modality is attractive since it makes no mention of possible worlds, and places no undue stress on our powers of imagination. It also has the appeal of being fashionable now that the notion of powers has been rediscovered in some contemporary metaphysical circles.[22] But the obvious objection to this line of thought is the well-worn but false claim that evolution-

[20] Book IX of the *Metaphysics* is the key source.
[21] In Aristotelian terminology, potentiality follows on actuality (*Metaphysics*, Book IX, ch. 8), and actuality is determined by essence.
[22] For an introduction to some of the issues relating to the metaphysics of powers see Michael Esfeld's "Humean metaphysics vs a metaphysics of powers" in *Time, Change and Reduction: Philosophical Aspects of Statistical Mechanics.* Ernst and Hütteman (eds) (Cambridge: Cambridge University Press, 2010, pp. 119–135. For more detailed discussions see

ary biology is incompatible with essentialism. I have argued at length elsewhere that this view is based on a misapprehension of the core claims of Aristotle's essentialism and the metaphysical alternatives, and that evolutionary biology actually presupposes Aristotelian essentialism.[23] But perhaps the main challenge facing this Aristotelian proposal is the difficulty of identifying biological essences. While many are now happy to recognise the periodic table of elements, say, as specifying the Aristotelian essences of the chemical elements, many are unsure that anything analogous is to be found in biology. But matters are not nearly as challenging on this score as they used to be now that geneticists have become comfortable with the notion of developmental programmes.

The development in view here is the process by which complex multicellular organisms are built from single cells. A developmental programme is the set of development control genes and their pattern of expression. Developmental control genes are genes that control the expression of other genes, 'switching' them on and off in a set sequence that terminates in the construction of the mature multicellular organism. It is the developmental programme, rather than the entire genome itself, which determines what sort of organism will ultimately be built from the original single cell.[24]

The Metaphysics of Powers, Marmodoro (ed.) (London: Routledge, 2010), and *Properties, Powers and Structures*, Bird, Ellis and Sankey (eds), (London: Routledge, 2011).

[23] See my "Can evolutionary biology do without essentialism?" in *Human Nature*. Royal Institute of Philosophy Supplement: 70 (Cambridge: Cambridge University Press, 2012, pp. 83–103) for an extended discussion of these points. See also Rejane Bernier, "The Species as Individual: Facing Essentialism", *Systematic Zoology*, Vol. 33, No. 4, 1984: 460–469, Dennis Walsh, "Evolutionary Essentialism", *Brit. J. Phil.Sci.* 57, 2006: 425–448, and Michael Devitt, "Resurrecting Biological Essentialism", *Philosophy of Science*, 75, 2008: 344–382.

[24] For an extended discussion of the biological details see Ch. 6 of Stearns and Hoekstra's *Evolution: An Introduction*. 2nd Ed. (Oxford: Oxford University Press, 2005). That developmental programmes might be the key to distinguishing biological species was raised over thirty years ago by King and Wilson in their "Evolution at two levels in humans and chimpanzees" *Science*, **188**, 1975: 107–166. Then the suggestion was used to account for the paradoxical fact that genetically human and chimpanzees are very similar while phenotypically very different. This suggestion has now received empirical support from various studies. The work of Khaitovich and Pääbo on primate gene expression offers a particularly clear example of how species specific variation in gene expression is now taken to be the distinguishing feature of a species. In particular see Philip Khaitovich, Wolfgang Enard, Michael Lachmann, Svante Pääbo "Evolution of primate gene expression", *Nature Reviews Genetics*, **7**, 2006: 693–702, Svante Pääbo, Philip Khaitovich et al, "Extension of cortical synaptic development distinguishes humans from chimpanzees and macaques", *Genome Research*, published online Feb 2, 2012. Interestingly enough, support for this view can even be found amongst philosophers of biology who are unsympathetic to essentialism. See John Dupré, *The Disorder of Things* (Cambridge Mass: Harvard University Press, 1993, p. 55).

Now the suggestion is to identify biological essences with species specific developmental programmes that maps genotypes onto phenotypes.[25] When this approach to biological essence is adopted the proposal with respect to modality takes the following form:

1. Potentiality is grounded in actuality, so all strictly biological possibilities must be grounded in some actual feature of this world.
2. What makes a biological form biologically necessary, possible or impossible are the essences of currently existing biological forms.
3. The essence of a biological form is its species specific developmental programme.
4. X is *biologically* possible if and only if x lies within the scope of the developmental programme of an actual organism. X is *biologically* impossible if it does not fall within the scope of the developmental programme of an actual organism. X is *biologically* necessary if the developmental programme of an actual organism cannot be completed without the occurrence of x.[26]
5. The other types of modality can then be characterised as follows: X is *physically* possible if it is not ruled out by the causal powers and liabilities of the formal objects of physics and chemistry, *physically* impossible if ruled out by these powers and liabilities, and *physically* necessary if it is a

---

[25] See my "Can evolutionary biology do without essentialism?" for discussion of this point.
[26] There are two ways in which x may fall within the scope of a developmental programme. The trajectory of a developmental programme is often affected by factors external to the organism. Certain environmental factors can influence the activity of control genes. Now if the actualisation of such external factors would lead a developmental programme down a particular path to x, then x falls within the scope of the developmental programme, and is biologically possible. But the trajectory of a developmental programme can be altered by a mutation on a control gene or by experimental perturbation. (The duplication of control genes is perhaps the most common mutation that opens up new developmental trajectories; manipulation of development by using colchicine to affect the activity of control genes is one example of experimental perturbation.) Since such mutations arise in the natural course of things, and particularly because we can now intervene in developmental processes, all that is required for the change in developmental programmes currently exists. This gives us a second sense in which x can fall within the scope of a developmental programme. If a single mutation on or perturbation of a control gene would lead a developmental programme down a particular path to x, then x falls within the scope of that programme, and is biologically possible.

consequence of these powers and liabilities. X is *absolutely* or *metaphysically* possible if it is not repugnant to being-qua-being, *absolutely* or *metaphysically* impossible if it is repugnant to being-qua-being, *absolutely* or *metaphysically* necessary if it is a consequence of being-qua-being. X is *logically* possible if it is consistent with the axioms of a given logical system, *logically* impossible if inconsistent with the axioms of that system, *logically* necessary if it is an axiom of that system or follows from the axioms of that system.

6. The specifically biological modal facts are to be discovered by the empirical investigation of developmental programmes, in particular by intervening in developmental processes.

Some implications of this approach are immediately obvious. First, the sorting of effects into the various biological modal categories will be done primarily by biologists, not metaphysicians. Second, morphospace is not stable, but changes as developmental programmes change. What was formerly biological possible may become biologically impossible because the relevant developmental programmes are now lost due to extinction. Trilobites are a case in point. Conversely, a current biological impossibility may become possible if the requisite developmental programme should arise. Most importantly however, what is conceivable or logically possible is not to be confused with biological possibility. And, of course, the physically possible may be biologically impossible. Trilobites, for example, remain physically possible (as well as logically and metaphysically possible) although they are now a biological impossibility. Finally, morphospace is quite large – larger than some structuralists allow, but much smaller than the neo-Darwinians and Gould have assumed.

However, the crucial point about this approach to modality for present purposes is it provides a principled method of sorting alternative effects according to their modal character. This in turn provides a way of adjudicating between the various explanations on offer for biological phenomena. If two biologists differ with respect to the explanatory cause they wish to appeal to to explain a given effect, one appealing to natural selection, say, another to physical constraints, we can make a start by sorting the actual and alternative effects according to their modal character the better to then determine which if any of the favoured causes is a suitable candidate. It is very likely that in the current state of information

CONTRASTIVE EXPLANATIONS IN EVOLUTIONARY BIOLOGY

we will not be in a position to carrying out the required sorting. But if we follow Aristotle's lead, at least we know what sorts of investigations will turn up the needed information. And that is progress.[27]

---

[27] I would like to express my thanks to David Oderberg for his many useful comments on early versions of this chapter.

5

ANIMATE BEINGS: THEIR NATURE AND IDENTITY

Gary S. Rosenkrantz

Abstract
Drawing inspiration from Aristotle's biological writings, I attempt to elucidate what it is for something to be alive by providing illuminating logically necessary and sufficient conditions for something's being a living thing in *the broadest sense.* I then propose a related account of identity conditions for *carbon-based* living organisms.

1. Introduction

I begin by stating three fundamental necessary truths about living things. First, an animate being is a concrete entity capable of living a life. Second, a life, or at least any contingent being's life, is a *process* consisting of a series of intrinsic changes in an animate being. Third, an animate being is *not* a process; such a being – at least of the most basic sort – is what was traditionally called an *individual substance.* In one ordinary sense of 'thing', synonymous with 'individual substance', it can be said, for instance, that a chameleon's changing color is not a *thing*; it is a change in one. A fourth proposition, that an animate being is *necessarily* an animate being, will be defended later.

Our *everyday conceptual scheme* includes a relatively basic conception of an *animate object* (as distinguished from an *inanimate object*). Moreover, there is a more theoretical biological conception of a *carbon-based living organism.* Lastly, there is an all-inclusive conception of an *animate being in the broadest sense.* Instances of the corresponding all-inclusive kind include *compound animate physical beings,* e.g., carbon-based living organisms and their living parts. Living organisms and their living parts are capable of living a *physical life,* a kind of life that typically involves metabolic and reproductive activities.

So far as we know, all living organisms are *carbon-based.*[1] Nevertheless, non-carbon-based living organisms cannot be excluded

---

[1] I use 'organism' in a sense *broader than* '[chemically] *organic* or carbon-based organism'. In one sense of 'organism', '*living* organism' is redundant and '*dead* organism' implicitly self-contradictory.

Classifying Reality, First Edition. Edited by David S. Oderberg. Copyright © 2013 The Authors. Book compilation © 2013 Blackwell Publishing Ltd.

as a possibility, though, given our current epistemic position, any conception we have of non-carbon-based living organisms must be based on their hypothesized resemblance to [carbon-based] living organisms. My account of life will be consistent with that possibility.

Some ancient peoples accepted the animistic notion that *every* object is animate on the ground that *every* object is capable of living a *mental life*. Of course, such notions are not widely accepted now and most contemporary folk do not think that electrons, carbon atoms, water molecules, pieces of iron, or tables are animate or capable of living a mental life.

However, it is widely believed that a variety of living organisms are capable of living a mental life, for instance, animals of various sorts, including human animals. But some living organisms apparently lack that capability, for instance, blades of grass. All *persons* have this capability.

Moreover, in the broadest sense of *animate*, it can be argued that it is metaphysically possible for there to be a person who is animate in virtue of its capability to live a mental life. Such a person might be conceived of as immaterial or non-physical; I have defended the metaphysical possibility (though not the actuality) of *non-physical souls* – non-compound, non-located mass-less persons.[2] And, it might be argued that it is metaphysically possible for there to be a person who is a self-conscious indivisible [*material*] particle, possessing volume and mass. Also, it might be argued that a person embodied in a *machine* such as a computer, robot, or the like, is metaphysically possible. Persons of the aforementioned sorts would not – or need not – be embodied in living organisms. My account of what it is for something to be alive will be logically consistent with the existence of such persons.

However, it appears that none of us can conceive of a life which is neither *physical* nor *mental*. Thus, it appears that in the broadest sense of *animate being*, necessarily, something is an animate being if and only if it is capable of living a physical life or a mental life.

Yet, given the profound differences between *embodied persons* of various sorts, *non-physical souls*, and *mindless living organisms*, it might be asked "Are they *literally* describable as *animate*, for

² Joshua Hoffman and Gary S. Rosenkrantz, *The Divine Attributes* (Oxford: Blackwell, 2002), chap. 3.

instance, in virtue of some common feature, or merely *metaphorically* so?" I shall argue that what they have in common can be elucidated via the notion of an activity which is *goal-directed* (or *end-directed*).

Examples of such goal-directed activities include intentional *psychological activities*, for instance, one's seeking pleasure, apparently purposeful *biological activities* such as the beating of an animal's heart, which can be said to have as a goal *the pumping of an animal's blood through its blood vessels*, other apparently purposive *behaviors* such as a spider's weaving a web, a bird's making a nest, a beaver's building a dam, a human's fashioning a tool, as well as seemingly purposeful activities of *organically created constructions* and *humanly designed artifacts*, e.g., a spider-web's entangling a fly, a thermostat's controlling the operation of a furnace. In contrast, it appears that non-psychological, non-biological, law-governed *physical* and *chemical* phenomena such as *mutual gravitational attraction* and *two atoms of hydrogen bonding with an atom of oxygen* are *not* goal-directed. The view that *all* law-governed activities in nature are goal-directed is highly implausible.[3]

As we shall see, a mindless living organism, an embodied person, or a non-physical soul, unlike an inanimate being, necessarily instantiates some *species of concrete individual substance* such that it is [metaphysically] possible for that species to have an instance that performs a goal-directed activity *of a certain kind*, which I shall call a *primary* goal-directed activity. To say that a concrete individual substance, x, performs a primary goal-directed activity is to say that x performs a goal-directed activity and there is *no* contingent being, y, such that: $y \neq x$ and y (or a part of y) begins to perform a goal-directed activity *prior to*, or *concurrently with*, x. It is necessarily the case that any animate beings of the aforementioned sorts *resemble* one another *in a fundamental respect* by virtue of necessarily instantiating a species of concrete individual substance that possibly has an instance that performs a primary goal-directed activity.

Various historically important disagreements in metaphysics concern whether the inanimate is causally prior to the animate

---

[3]   Cf. George Molnar, *Powers: A Study in Metaphysics*, edited by Stephen Mumford (Oxford: Oxford University Press, 2003). Molnar argues that a physical disposition, e.g., *salt's water-solubility*, has *physical intentionality*, directed upon its actuator, e.g., *water*. Such *object-directedness* appears insufficient for *goal-directedness* [of the salient kind(s) various biological and psychological activities exemplify].

(and whether every psychological activity derives from some physical activity), or whether the animate is causally prior to the inanimate (and whether every physical activity derives from some psychological activity). My account of what it is to be an animate being aims to be neutral with respect to these disagreements, for instance, disagreements between materialists and idealists and between materialists and Cartesian dualists. *A fortiori*, this account aims to be neutral about the disagreement over whether the goal-directedness of psychological activities derives from the goal-directedness of physical activities or vice versa.

Every living organism lives a physical life, though not every being that lives a physical life is a living organism. In particular, specialized living parts of multi-cellular organisms, for instance, human lung cells, lungs, and respiratory systems may be said to live a physical life, but are not themselves living organisms. The distinction between living organisms and such living parts appears to be real, not conventional, and to be grounded in the natural evolutionary causal priority of the former to the latter.

I believe that *collectives* like ant colonies, symbiotically interrelated organisms, human societies, and ecosystems are not compound individual substances because they lack the required *mereological unity*, much as pairs of unattached particles are not *physical objects*.[4] For similar reasons, I doubt that collectives of the aforementioned sorts are animate beings (e.g., organisms or "super-organisms").

2. Natural Kinds and Ontological Categories

I shall argue that the question "What is an animate being?" can be answered by *quantifying over ontological categories* and *natural kinds*.[5] Relevant conceptions of an ontological category and of a natural kind go back to Aristotle.

---

[4] Another way in which a [concrete] collective differs from a compound individual substance is that, at some level, it is composed of parts that *don't* belong to the same species of concrete entity as it does: necessarily, at some level, a collective is composed of non-collectives, whereas, necessarily, a compound individual substance is composed of individual substances. (In the relevant sense of 'composition', physical composition entails the possibility of physical decomposition.) For related arguments that [concrete] collectives and aggregates aren't individual substances see Joshua Hoffman and Gary S. Rosenkrantz, *Substance: Its Nature and Existence* (London: Routledge, 1997), pp. 69–72.

[5] In chap. 2 of *Substance: Its Nature and Existence*, Joshua Hoffman and I argue that the concepts of *concrete entity* and *individual substance* can be elucidated via quantification over ontological categories.

The phrase 'natural kind of compound physical object' and the more traditional phrase 'natural kind of compound physical [concrete individual] substance' are co-referential. *Piece of gold, atom of hydrogen, molecule of DNA,* and *carbon-based living thing* – the *summum genus* of Biology – are examples of such natural kinds, but *not* the *species* and *genera* of contemporary Biology.[6]

Every such natural kind, K, is such that: (i) it is impossible that something instantiates K *contingently,* (ii) K is a proper object of inquiry in natural science, (iii) K figures in one or more natural laws, (iv) K is *possibly* instantiated in the absence of an intention or belief of a *contingent being* that an instance of K is *for* performing some goal-directed activity, (v) K supervenes on structural and compositional properties, i.e., necessarily, for any x & y, if x instantiates K and x & y have the same structural and compositional properties, then y instantiates K, and (vi) K places limits on the *kinds of parts* an instance of K could have.

Although natural kinds of compound *physical stuff,* e.g., water, are not kinds of *physical object,* they can be characterized along the same lines. Moreover, while a natural kind of either sort *possibly* has an instance that exists *naturally,* such a kind also may *fail* to have a naturally existing instance, e.g., synthetic fabrics of various natural kinds likely do not exist in nature. A corollary is that *carbon-based living organism* being a natural kind is compatible with a carbon-based living organism [of the most elementary sort] being created *synthetically.* However, *artifact kinds,* for instance, *table, statue,* do not satisfy (at least) necessary condition (iv) of a natural kind, stated above, and therefore, are not natural kinds. Also, some process-kinds are artificial, e.g., *push-up,* and others are natural, e.g., *combustion.*

Ontological categories are the more general and/or basic kinds of being, for instance, *concrete entity, abstract entity.* Other examples include *species* of concrete entity: *individual substance, event, place, time, boundary, collection* (or *individual sum*), and *species* of abstract entity: *property, relation, set,* and *proposition.* Some species of the latter categories, for instance, *physical substance* and *spiritual substance,* are themselves ontological categories. Elsewhere,[7] I

[6] See Gary S. Rosenkrantz, 'What is Life?' in Tian Yu Cao (Ed.) *Proceedings of the Twentieth World Congress of Philosophy* Vol. 10: Philosophy of Science, (Bowling Green, O.: Philosophy Documentation Center, 2001), pp. 125–134.
[7] 'Ontological Categories' in Tuomas Takho (Ed.) *Contemporary Aristotelian Metaphysics* (Cambridge: Cambridge University Press, 2012).

attempt to elucidate the broadest notion of an ontological category by enumerating 10 necessary conditions for any well-formed predicate '*F*' to express a category of this kind *without gratuitous logical complexity or redundancy*.[8] These conditions include *that there might be an F*,[9] and *that it is impossible for something to be F contingently*.

Natural, *artificial*, and *social kinds* are not general or basic enough to be ontological categories; like ontological categories, they stand in species-genus relations to other kinds, e.g., *deuterium* is a species of *hydrogen*, *colonial* is a species of *house*, and *spontaneous market* is a species of *social entity*, respectively. Unlike instances of natural kinds of compound physical objects, instances of artificial or social kinds are existentially dependent upon psychological activities of contingent beings. Necessarily, an instance of an artificial kind has an *artificial goal-directed function*, e.g., a screw-driver is *for driving screws*. Social and natural kinds necessarily lack such instances.

My intuition is that, *necessarily, whatever dies, ceases to exist*. Evidently, this entails that an animate being is *necessarily* an animate being. If an animate being is necessarily an animate being, then *carbon-based living organism* qualifies as a natural kind of compound physical object, and a *carbon-based living organism* cannot be identified with the *corpse* that remains after it dies. A conflicting intuition is that such organisms can survive their deaths by becoming corpses, and hence, are *contingently* alive. The relevant linguistic evidence appears inconclusive. For instance, we say 'After Fido *passed away* we buried his *remains*', but also 'Fido *is* dead and buried'; apparently, the former implies that Fido ceased to exist when he died, the latter that Fido exists *post-mortem*.

However, the foregoing controversy is fundamentally *metaphysical*, not linguistic. The following extremely plausible metaphysical modal principle concerning [maximally] *general scientific kinds* supports my intuition.

---

[8]   Replace the schematic letter '*F*' with an appropriate predicate expression.
[9]   For the purposes of ontological neutrality, it's advantageous to read 'might' as expressing *epistemic possibility*, i.e., consistency with everything we know. For other purposes, it may be advantageous to read 'might' as expressing metaphysical possibility, or to replace (1) with '(1′) (∃x) (x is F)'.

The *summum genus* of any *abstract* or *natural science* (other than their *sub-sciences*, e.g., botany, zoology)[10] is an *ontological category* or *natural kind* that is *necessarily* instantiated by whatever instantiates it and such that its instances are *the core subject-matter* of the science in question and its laws.

Apparent instances of this principle are *number, physical thing, chemical,* and [carbon-based] *living thing,* the *summum genera* of arithmetic, physics, chemistry, and biology, respectively. I conclude that [carbon-based] living thing is a natural kind, and a *necessary property* of whatever instantiates it.

It might be replied that the *summum genus* of biology is an *organic chemical structure* necessarily instantiated by living and dead things *alike*. This reply entails that *dead things* are part of the *core* subject-matter of biology. But, *necessarily*, a corpse *results from* a living thing dying, but in general, a living thing does *not* result from a corpse reviving. Thus, living things are *causally prior* to dead things in a very strong sense. Furthermore, any natural law concerning dead things *not* relating them to living things is *non-biological*. Hence, the core subject-matter of biology is *living things* and dead things are *at most* a part of its *peripheral* subject-matter. I conclude that the foregoing possible reply is unpersuasive.

3. Activities of Animate Beings

Three sorts of activities are intimately associated with animate beings: *metabolic, reproductive,* and *psychological* activities. Some living organisms, for instance, mules, and some living parts of organisms, for instance, leucocytes, are incapable of reproduction. While all psychologically active beings are alive, it appears that some living organisms are incapable of psychological activity. However, quite credibly, it is a necessary truth justifiable *a priori* that *non-mental life,* for instance, life as conceived from a biological perspective, involves metabolic activity, namely, a living thing's actively adding/subtracting parts, e.g., the replacement of

---

[10] I would argue that any sub-kind, *K*, of carbon-based living organism, e.g., *oak-kind, animal-kind,* possibly has a *marginal* instance, *i,* such that *i possibly* mutates when coming into existence, resulting in *i*'s being of a kind, *K**, incompatible with *K*. In that case, *K* could be *contingently* instantiated by a living organism, and hence, doesn't qualify as either an *ontological category* or a *natural kind of compound physical substance.*

damaged/lost parts, growth, weight loss. After all, our *presumptive conception* of what constitutes *non-mental life* appears to be *abstracted* [in part] from everyday and/or scientific observations of the metabolic activity of living things, and there does *not* appear to be any good reason *to change* this conception.

To define metabolism and reproduction in a suitably general fashion, let '*x*' range over persisting compound physical objects and persisting compound entities which could be parts of them: *x* has *metabolic activity* over a period of time *t* just when throughout *t*, *x* continually changes its physical parts, where causes within *x* sustain this process of mereological change; *x reproduces* just when powered by its metabolism, *x* produces or co-produces something which co-instantiates a natural kind with *x*.

By *metabolic related activity* I mean either metabolic activity or activity which *causally contributes* to it, for instance, respiration, elimination. Similarly, by *reproductive related activity* I mean either reproduction or activity which causally contributes to it, for instance, mitosis, meiosis.

I won't attempt to define the intuitive notion of a psychological activity; it appears that we are directly acquainted with activities of this kind. Our conception of mental life appears to be abstracted [at least in part] from our direct experiences of such activities. Apparently, one can know *a priori* that, necessarily, mental life involves psychological activity.

Given that, necessarily, mental life involves psychological activity and non-mental life involves metabolic activity, I conclude that, necessarily, life involves psychological or metabolic activity.

Below, I defend the controversial view that viruses are inanimate. Because viruses lack a cellular structure and consist of a nucleic acid molecule, RNA or DNA, coated with protein, they are incapable of performing the most fundamental life-functions associated with carbon-based living organisms. In particular, viruses are incapable of self-maintenance, internally caused growth, or catabolism (*destructive metabolism*). In other words, they lack the capability for metabolic activity of any sort. Although some viruses appear to actively change their parts by injecting their nucleic acid molecules into organisms, this injection is a *sporadic* "one-shot" affair and cannot be continued. A chance genetic mutation of a particular kind is a second sort of sporadic change of a virus's parts that cannot be continued. Such sporadic changes are *not* metabolic activity. Moreover, it is apparent that a virus is incapable of psychological activity. Given that a virus isn't capable of either metabolic or psychological activity, a virus is incapable of living *a life*, a process consisting of a series of intrinsic changes of a relevant sort. I conclude that a virus isn't an animate being. Parallel arguments apply to other even smaller infectious organic pathogens, for instance, *viroids*, *virusoids*, and *prions*. A virus being inanimate is compatible with the fact that viruses evolve via natural selection, and with the fact that parts of contemporary viruses carry out goal-directed activities facilitating viral replication, for instance, placing a molecule of nucleic acid inside of a living organism. It should be noted that since a virus lacks metabolism, viral replication does not qualify as 'reproduction' in my sense.

Richard Dawkins has called such *mind-dependent* entities as religious ideas, languages, jokes, melodies, and fashions *memes*. One version of Social Darwinism contends that memes are *alive* on the grounds that, *like viruses*, they *spread*, in this instance, *from one mind to another*, and *evolve*, in this case, *culturally*. However, as we have seen, even though viruses *spread from one living organism to another* and *evolve via a process of natural selection*, they do *not* appear to be alive. Indeed, as with viruses, there is no apparent reason to believe that memes are capable of metabolic or psychological activity, and hence, there is no apparent reason to believe that memes are alive. So, *even if* the analogy with viruses is apt, it does not support the contention that memes are animate beings. Rather, it appears permissible to describe a meme as *living* or as *dead* just when the description is a *metaphorical* usage reflecting a meme's degree of currency among *living things*, for instance, *living languages* are those which are currently in general use within a sufficiently large linguistic community and *dead languages* are those which are not. Yet other metaphorical usages of 'life' – or its cognates – based on different analogies, are *the* [half] *life of a radioactive isotope, the Sun's life, a live* [electrified] *wire*, and so on.

Some argue that so-called *artificial life* [as instantiated by a computer program such that, when it runs, models the behavior of a population of living organisms and their evolution] qualifies as an animate being of some sort. But instances of such "artificial life" appear to lack the capability for metabolic or psychological activity, and thus, appear not to be alive. So, on reflection, it appears that an instance of such "artificial life" is a mere *simulation* of organic life and not *real life* of any sort.

4. An Account of the Concept of an Animate Being

Many despair of providing illuminating logically necessary and sufficient conditions for the concept of an animate being. Some, finding themselves unable to identify a set of such conditions, infer that this concept is *unintelligible* or, at least, *intolerably mysterious*. But, even given the variety of animate beings acknowledged as conceivable, I shall argue that this concept can be made tolerably clear, though needless to say, not absolutely precise, by providing a set of conditions of the aforementioned kind. Apparently, the discovery of such a set of conditions would have intrinsic value – *qua* analytical insight – and instrumental value, for instance, as a reply to an antirealist of the foregoing sort.

I now turn in earnest to elucidating the concept of an animate being via the notion of a goal-directed activity. It appears that, necessarily, for any x & y, if $x \neq y$ and x's having a capability to perform a goal-directed activity is explicable in terms of y, then x's having such a capability is ultimately explicable in terms of either a generative physical process of natural selection, e.g., Darwinian evolution, or a generative psychological activity, e.g., intelligent design. Alternatively, x's having a capability of this kind may be inexplicable, or on some views be self-explanatory, e.g., if x = God.

Drawing on Larry Wright's influential work, I have argued that the *goal-directedness* of a biological activity of a living organism (or a part of one), although an *ineliminable* feature of such an activity, is nonetheless *reducible* to a feature of an evolutionary natural selective process which is *altogether free of goal-directedness*.[11] In particular, I have defended the reductionist view that such an activity is goal-directed just when the trait of having the capability to perform such an activity was *naturally selected* in a living organism, or else naturally selected in one or more ancestor-organisms from whom a living organism inherited that trait via some line of descent. This reductionist view entails that a first living organism (or a part of one) didn't perform a goal-directed activity.

However, it might be objected to the reductionist view that, *possibly*, a *protobiont*, that is, an elementary [single-celled] first living organism, was such that it (or a part of it) was capable of performing a goal-directed activity by virtue of *pre-biotic* natural selection among self-replicating macromolecules. Or a theist

---

[11]   *Substance: Its Nature and Existence.*

might object to this reductionist view that a first living organism (or a part of one) was capable of performing a goal-directed activity in virtue of its being designed by, God, an animate being who has necessary existence. Regardless of whether such objections to the reductionist view are sound, the following assumption, which that view entails, is extremely plausible.

It is metaphysically possible that at a past time, t, there was an animate being, x, such that: x (or a part of x) performed a *primary* goal-directed activity at t.

In defending my account of the concept of an animate being I presuppose this metaphysical possibility, but not the reductionist view.

In my view, God would be an animate being who performed a primary goal-directed activity, as would a *first living organism* designed by God. Another example is provided by the possibility of a primeval living organism, among the first to have had a naturally selected trait of the requisite sort, and which itself descended from a protobiont, o, such that neither o nor any of its parts performed a goal-directed activity. It is plausible that *possibly* such a protobiont originated by *self-assembly* from parts none of which performed a goal-directed activity.

Apparently, any conceivable living organism is a *compound physical object* of a *natural kind* that possibly has naturally selected instances having *goal-directed metabolic and reproductive activities*. Accordingly, any conceivable *non-carbon-based* natural kind of living organism, like the familiar carbon-based natural kind, possibly has such instances, though, of course, their *compositional nature*, and some physical laws pertaining to this nature which govern their life activities, would differ from carbon-based living organisms.

My attempt to provide illuminating logically necessary and sufficient conditions for the concept of an animate being is based on definitions of two further preliminary technical notions, namely, the notions of *a primary living being* and *a secondary living being*.

(**D1**) x is a primary living being =df. (i) x is capable of metabolic or psychological activity, & (ii) x is an instance of one or more categories or natural kinds which are *species* of the category of *concrete individual substance*, & (iii) every such category or kind [instantiated by *x*] *possibly* has an instance, *y*, such that *y* (or a part of *y*) performs a *primary goal-directed activity* which is metabolic related, reproductive related, or psychological, & (iv) *x* is possibly not a proper part of something that satisfies (i)–(iii) above.

Earlier, the meanings and extensions of the key terms of conditions (i)–(iii) in **D1** were explained and surveyed. Note that because condition (iii) of **D1** does *not* require that *all* primary living beings are capable of performing goal-directed activities, **D1** allows for the possibility of protobionts which are *not* so capable. Concerning recursive condition (iv) of **D1**, it should be noted that, necessarily, a living organism (or a person) is possibly not a *part* of *another* living organism or person.

Every instance of the natural kind of compound physical object, *carbon-based living organism*, satisfies **D1**, e.g., paramecia, maple trees, lions; likewise for every instance of the conceivably broader kind *living organism*. Furthermore, the ontological category *nonphysical soul* is a species of concrete individual substance such that *every* instance of that category satisfies **D1**; likewise for any natural kind or ontological category instantiated by a person who is an indivisible or mass-less *physical object*. On some views, *persons* are *essentially* persons. On those views, *person* is an ontological category and a species of concrete individual substance such that *every* instance of that category satisfies **D1**. I would argue that any such person satisfies condition (iii) of **D1** in virtue of the metaphysical *possibility* of a person who is indivisible or lacks mass and who performs a primary goal-directed psychological activity.[12] On the other hand, if persons who are embodied in living organisms are essentially living organisms, but *contingently* persons, then *person* is *not* an ontological category.

Artifacts, for instance, screwdrivers, appear to be inanimate objects. I argue below that such ostensible physical objects are not primary living beings per **D1**.

An artifact would instantiate the ontological category *artifact* as well as a more specific non-natural artifact-kind, e.g., *screwdriver*. Moreover, *necessarily*, for any artifact-kind, *K*, and any goal-directed activity, *e*, performed by an instance, *x*, of *K*, at a time *t*,

12 I have defended the metaphysical possibility of non-physical persons; see note 2. This apparent possibility is consistent with the claim that persons are *essentially* persons, and therefore, *essentially* capable of *mental activities* of various sorts.

x performs e at t only if at t or earlier, there exists a *contingent being*, y, such that $y \neq x$ and y believes that a thing of kind K is *for* being used to achieve a relevant goal. Since beliefs are goal-directed activities, generally directed toward *truth* as a goal, it follows that no *possible instance* of the category *artifact* – a species of concrete individual substance – performs a primary goal-directed activity. Furthermore, necessarily, a *part* of an artifact performs a goal-directed activity only if that part is an artifact. Hence, *artifacts* do not satisfy condition (iii) of **D1**.

It is a *category mistake* to think that an artificially constructed person embodied in a machine, for instance, a computer, a robot, or the like, would be an [animate] artifact. After all, unlike an artifact, such a person *possibly* exists in the absence of an intention or belief that it is *for* performing some goal-directed activity, e.g., it might be constructed simply to create a synthetic person. For parallel reasons, *no* animate being, not even one intentionally created *for* performing some goal-directed activity, can be identified with an artifact, though an animate being can *be treated* as if it were one.

A synthetic person, *S*, of the sort in question satisfies **D1** for the following reasons. Since *S* would not be an artifact, it is evident that *S* either would instantiate a natural kind, *N*, of compound physical object, or else, would instantiate an ontological category which is a species of concrete individual substance and which is incompatible with *artifact*, for instance, *person*. Given earlier arguments, it is evident that every instance of any such ontological category would satisfy **D1**. On the other hand, while it appears likely that *N*, like natural kinds of synthetic fabric, would *not* have a naturally occurring instance, *N* would *possibly* have a naturally occurring instance that performs a primary goal-directed psychological activity, and thus, any instance of *N* would satisfy (iii) of **D1**, along with the other conditions in **D1**.

Ostensible physical objects of a variety of other natural kinds appear to be *inanimate*, e.g., *electron* (a natural kind of non-compound object), *piece of iron*, *water molecule*, *glacier* (natural kinds of compound object). It can be plausibly argued that such physical objects are not primary living beings per **D1**. In particular, given that such physical objects are incapable of psychological activity, each of them instantiates a natural kind that does *not* possibly have an instance that is capable of performing a *goal-directed activity*, and consequently, such physical objects do not satisfy condition (iii) of **D1**.

I turn next to living [possible] proper parts of living organisms such as a living heart cell, heart, or circulatory system. A living being of this kind is *not* an instance of an ontological category or natural kind which is a species of concrete individual substance and which possibly has an instance that performs a *primary* goal-directed activity. Therefore, it fails to satisfy condition (iii) of **D1**.

Let us now consider **D1** in relation to the curious case of proteinoid microspheres discovered by Sidney Fox. When certain amino acids are heated together on a slab of volcanic rock at 130° centigrade, they are apt to copolymerize, producing the peptide *proteinoid*. When this "mini-protein" is immersed in seawater, durable proteinoid microspheres self-assemble. Intriguingly, as these micropheres absorb proteinoid from their watery surroundings they grow and bud, manifesting rudimentary *metabolic* and *reproductive* capabilities. Their metabolic and reproductive activities become more robust when ATP is introduced into the surroundings. Fox hypothesized that proteinoid microspheres are elementary living organisms.[13]

However, a proteinoid microsphere is not comparable in complexity to recognized living organisms, and in particular, does *not* have as a part a nucleic acid or "self-replicable" carbon-based macromolecule. Thus, unlike recognized living organisms, a proteinoid microsphere is incapable of inheriting variations, and so, lacks *heredity*. Hence, it appears that a proteinoid microsphere is *not* a living organism.[14]

I shall argue, similarly, that a proteinoid microsphere is not a primary living being per **D1**. First, it can be argued plausibly that such a microsphere is an instance of the *natural kind* [of compound physical object] *proteinoid microsphere* (henceforth, **PM**). The possible instances of **PM** are necessarily composed of proteinoid assembled in a sphere-like way, and hence, they necessarily do not have a "self-replicable" macromolecule as a part. Hence, these possible instances necessarily lack heritable variations. Moreover, it is highly plausible that if there *were* a natural kind, **PM***, whose instances had *as parts* an instance of **PM** *and* some integrally related macromolecular hereditary mechanism, then **PM*** and **PM** would figure in very different natural laws. But, if so,

[13] Sidney Fox, *The Emergence of Life* (New York: Basic Books, 1988).
[14] Biologist John Maynard Smith has argued that proteinoid microspheres are not living organisms on these grounds. See his *The Problems of Biology* (Oxford: Oxford University Press, 1986), p. 114. I shall advance an importantly different version of such an argument.

then **PM*** (and its instances) would be other than **PM** (and its instances). I conclude that it is impossible for instances of **PM** to evolve by natural selection. Furthermore, the activities of self-assembled instances of **PM** (including their parts' activities), e.g., the metabolic and reproductive related activities of those instances, are apparently *not* goal-directed. Accordingly, it appears that no possible instance of **PM** has a *primary goal-directed activity*, and hence, that no instance of **PM** *satisfies* condition (iii) of **D1**. I conclude that a proteinoid microsphere is not a primary living being per **D1**.

On the other hand, it is not obviously impossible for a proteinoid microsphere to be a *proper part* of a primary living being [of some natural kind, presumably *carbon-based living organism*], and for such a proteinoid microsphere to perform goal-directed metabolic and/or reproductive related activities as a result of the natural selection of *primary living beings* of that natural kind. Since a hypothetical part of this sort would have a capability for metabolic activity and perform goal-directed activities, it would appear to be alive; it might be a minimalistic case of a "secondary living being."[15]

(**D2**) *x* is a secondary living being =df. (i) *x* is possibly a proper part of a primary living being, & (ii) *x* is capable of metabolic activity, & (iii) *x* is an instance of a *natural kind* which is *necessarily* such that: (for any *y*, if *y* is an instance of that kind, then *y* [or a proper part of *y*] is capable of performing goal-directed activities which are metabolic or reproductive related, and *y* [or that proper part] exercises that capability at a time *t* only if a primary living being [or a proper part of one] performs goal-directed activities at a time *t'* not later than *t*.)

Ostensible physical objects of a variety of artifact and natural kinds discussed earlier, whose instances seem to be inanimate, apparently fail to satisfy condition (iii) of **D2**. In particular, artifacts do not instantiate a natural kind, and the instances of the natural kinds in question appear to be incapable of performing goal-directed activities of the requisite sort.

---

[15] Red blood cells appear to be [weakly] metabolically active living [possible] proper parts of organisms, *not* themselves organisms, which perform goal-directed metabolic related activities and which don't have a nucleic acid or "self-replicable" macromolecule as a part.

But, as I shall argue below, living skin cells, hearts, appendixes, and nervous systems satisfy **D2**. Let us call such a [possible] proper part of a carbon-based living organism a *living* [possible] *part* for short. Although no living part is an organism, under certain circumstances, some living parts can survive and reproduce *apart* from an organism, e.g., in a tissue culture. Because every living part is possibly a proper part of a primary living being, every living part satisfies (i) of *D2*. Moreover, since every living part is *capable of metabolic activity*, every living part satisfies (ii) of *D2*. Additionally, a living part is a natural thing, and a natural thing's *causal powers*, including those of any of its parts, correspond to some natural kind it instantiates. For instance, living parts instantiate natural kinds like [*carbon-based living*] *skin cell, nerve cell, bone cell,* etc. Furthermore, *necessarily,* every living part (or at least a *part* of one) is capable of performing *specialized goal-directed* activities of the requisite sort and *exercises* such a causal power at a time *t only if* a *primary living being* (or a part of one) performs goal-directed activities at some time *t′* not later than *t*.[16] Hence, every living part satisfies (iii) of **D2** *qua* its instantiation of some natural kind. I conclude that every living part is a secondary living being per **D2**.

D3, below, provides the promised set of necessary and sufficient conditions for the concept of an animate being.

(**D3**) *x* is an animate being =df. *x* is a primary living being or a secondary living being.

5. Suspended Animation

My account is applicable to the equivocal case of certain insects which can be freeze-dried and revived later via rehydration with warm water. It is natural to say that the insect is in a state of *suspended animation* while freeze-dried, a state which, unlike *death*, is *reversible*. In death, an organism's capability for metabolic activity is irreversibly lost, whereas in suspended animation, although an organism loses this capability, this loss is reversible. Both death

---

[16]   A vestigial organ may no longer be capable of performing goal-directed activities, but it has *parts* that are so capable, e.g., organelles which are parts of its cells and which are capable of performing goal-directed metabolic or reproductive related activities.

and suspended animation should be distinguished from a state of *dormancy* or *stasis* in which metabolic activity ceases, but the capability for metabolic activity remains. However, the insect's being in a state of *suspended animation*, taken *literally*, entails that the insect is *inanimate* while freeze-dried. Because *being animate* is a necessary characteristic of whatever has it, such a literal reading, while seemingly natural, entails that the living organism in question *exists intermittently* over the course of the aforementioned process. While it is understandable that some will find this consequence odd, I am nonetheless inclined to accept it for two reasons. First, to uphold the *particular intuition* that there are *literally* cases of suspended animation, e.g., that the insect is an *inanimate being* while freeze-dried. Second, to uphold the *metaphysical theory* that there are two basic kinds of *compound physical objects* having clashing causal principles of *mereological unity*: *inanimate pieces of matter*, whose parts are united via iterated *joining* relations (involving a dynamic equilibrium of attractive and repulsive fundamental physical forces), and *carbon-based living organisms*, whose parts are functionally united in virtue of a molecularly encoded microstructural hereditary "blueprint" and the causal activity of a "master-part," e.g., a central nervous system, which *controls* the biological functions of such an organism's parts.[17]

On the other hand, if a living organism's existing intermittently is unacceptable, it can be argued that the freeze-dried insect is an *animate being* by arguing that it has a *potentiality* for metabolic activity in a sense different from a *capability* for such activity as understood above.

In particular, **D1–D3** can readily be understood so as to accommodate *either* the intuition that a freeze-dried insect is an inanimate being, *or* the intuition that a freeze-dried insect is an animate being, depending on how 'capable' in **D1** is understood. Clearly, in one sense of *capable*, a freeze-dried insect is *not* capable of metabolic activity. Roughly speaking, to say that such an insect, *i*, is capable of metabolic activity *before i is freeze-dried* is to say that, *before i is freeze-dried*, *i* has a physical structure, *S1*, such that it is *physically possible* that *i* has metabolic activity while it has *S1*, and to say that *i* is incapable of metabolic activity *after i is freeze-dried* is to

---

[17]   See Joshua Hoffman and Gary S. Rosenkrantz, 'On the Unity of Compound Things: Living and Non-Living' *Ratio* 11 (1998), pp. 289–315, *Substance: Its Nature and Existence*, pp. 73–149; also see section VI below.

say that, *after i is freeze-dried, i* has a different physical structure, *S2*, such that it is *physically impossible* that *i* has metabolic activity while it has *S2*.

In the sense of *capable* in question, a rubber ball, *b*, under ordinary conditions at a time *t*, is capable of *bouncing*, but *not* of *shattering*, in virtue of the physical structure, *S**, had by *b* at *t*, and the same rubber ball immersed in liquid nitrogen, at a time *t**, is capable of *shattering*, but *not* of *bouncing*, in virtue of the different physical structure, *S***, had by *b* at *t**. A capability in this sense can be described as a *first-order capability*. Yet, it might be said that in another sense of capability, i.e., that of a *higher-order capability* or a *potentiality*, even when immersed in liquid nitrogen at *t**, *b* has the potential to bounce, and even under ordinary conditions at *t*, *b* has the potential to shatter, because at the relevant times, it is physically possible for *b* to *change* its physical structure from *S*** to *S**, and from *S** to *S***, respectively. If we understand 'capability' in **D1** to mean a *first-order capability*, then **D3** entails that a freeze-dried insect does not qualify as an animate being. On the other hand, if we understand 'capability' in **D1** to mean a *higher-order capability* or *potentiality*, then **D3** is compatible with a freeze-dried insect qualifying as an animate being. So, apparently, one imprecision in our concept of a *living organism* reflects another imprecision in our concept of a *capability*.

6. The Identity of Carbon-based Living Organisms

I now argue that the identity of a carbon-based living organism, *O*, is best understood as a function of the identity of its *master-part*, a proper part which is uniquely *vital*, *essential*, and *controlling* (or regulatory), as explicated in **D4–D8** below.

(**D4**) *P* is a *vital part* of *O* at a time *t* = df. (i) at *t*, *P* is a proper part of *O*, & (ii) at *t*, *P* performs a biological function, *F*, such that it is physically necessary that, if, at *t*, *P* were *permanently* to cease performing *F*, and there were nothing performing *F* in place of *P*, then *O* would cease to be alive at *t* (or else *very shortly* thereafter – relative to the maximum life-span of organisms of *O*'s species).

(**D5**) *P* is an *essential part* of *O* = df. (i) *P* is a proper part of *O*, & (ii) it is impossible that *O* exists and lacks *P* as a part.

For instance, central nervous systems are vital and essential, stomachs vital but inessential. The time-lag between the destruction of the *stomach* and death, and the apparent lack of a time-lag between the destruction of the *central nervous system* and death, is best explained via this distinction.

(**D6**) A biological function, *F1*, of a part, *P1*, of *O controls* a biological function, *F2*, of a part, *P2*, of *O* from a time, *t1*, up to a later time, *t2* = df. (i) *P2* engages in an activity, ø-ing,[18] such that: from *t1* up to *t2*, *P2* performs *F2* by ø-ing, & (ii) there are one or more ranges, $R_1 \ldots R_n$, of numerical measures of the biologically relevant way(s) in which *P2* øs, where each such range is numerically ordered by magnitude from a minimum to a maximum value and where it is *physically possible* that *P2*'s ø-ing has each such measure, & (iii) at any time *t* in the interval from *t1* up to *t2*, *P1*'s performing *F1* causes *P2*'s ø-ing to have a measure, M_1, that falls within a sub-range of R_1[19] [& parallel-wise with respect to *P2*'s ø-ing and $R_2 \ldots R_n$].

Fido's heart, *h*, biologically functions to *pump blood* by *beating* with a numerically measurable *rate* and *force*. Fido's central nervous system functions to control (as in **D6**) every biological function of *h*, and of Fido's other parts, by *causing* the relevant measures of Fido's biological activities (e.g., *heart rate, blood pressure, metabolic rate*) to fall within certain *ranges*. Apparently, no other proper part of Fido has this causal role. Analogously, a thermostat's temperature-controlling activity *causes* temperatures to fall within a certain range and no other proper part of the heating/cooling system in question has that role.

(**D7**) *P* is *O*'s master-part at a time *t* = df. (i) *P* is a vital part of *O* at *t*, & (ii) *P* is an essential part of *O* at *t*, & (iii) for any biological function, *F*, of a part of *O*, *P* has the biological function of controlling *F*.

Apparent examples of master-parts include a mammal's *central nervous system*, an insect's *nervous system*, a jellyfish's *neural net*, a unicellular, myriad-nucleated, [*plasmodial*] slime mold's *nuclear*

---

[18]   Replace the schematic letter 'ø' with an appropriate verb expression.
[19]   A 'sub-range of R_1' means either a *proper* sub-range of R_1 which excludes one or both of R_1's limiting measures, i.e., their minimum and maximum values, or an *improper* sub-range of R_1, i.e., R_1 itself.

system,[20] an amoeba's *nucleus*, and a bacterium's *nucleoid* (containing DNA and RNA). Such examples *inductively confirm* that *every* carbon-based living organism has a master-part.

Plants apparently lack a *centralized* master-part. Since a plant's (*P*'s) sap is produced and maintained by *P* and performs a vital life-function controlled by *P*, *P*'s sap appears to be *part* of *P*. *Something* other than *P*'s sap controls *P*'s life-functions. However, I have no reason to believe that *P*'s sap is part of the controller or that *P*'s roots, stems, and leaves are not. So, I suspect that *P*'s [*decentralized*] master-part is *P minus its sap*. Parallel remarks apply to a sponge, which is composed of *specialized cellular layers* and a *fluid* between them.

One controversial case is a *pseudoplasmodium*, composed of a myriad of massed, unicellular, mono-nucleated, cooperating [*cellular*] slime molds. It manifests goal-directed behavior and some cells in the mass develop *specialized reproductive-related functions*, suggesting a *multi-cellular organism*; yet, the individual cells in the mass are capable of *living independently under natural conditions*, suggesting, rather, a *collective* of "social" *unicellular organisms*. (Two examples of *multi-cellular* "social" organisms are ants and bees.) The Hoffman/Rosenkrantz account of a [carbon-based] living organism's mereological unity, described in section 5, entails that a pseudoplasmodium is a *multi-cellular organism* just if it has a master-part; but it is not apparent that it has one.

I propose the following criterion of identity for carbon-based living organisms.

(**D8**) Necessarily, a carbon-based living organism *O* at time *t* = a carbon-based living organism *O** at time *t** if and only if *O*'s master-part at *t* = *O**'s master-part at *t**.

Three applications of **D8** are described below.

(1) *This* caterpillar = *that* butterfly just when the latter has the same nervous system as the former. (2) The sap of a plant, *Pl*, is drained and replaced with the sap of another plant grown from a cutting of *Pl*. *Pl*'s original sap was a vital but inessential part of *Pl*. On the assumption that *Pl*'s master-part is *Pl* minus its sap, **D8** has

---

[20] Such a unicellular slime mold is formed by the *fusion* of a myriad of independently living mono-nucleated cells; the *simultaneous division* of such a unicellular slime mold's myriad nuclei during reproduction evidences a functionally integrated *nuclear system*.

the intuitively plausible consequence that *Pl* survives the replacement of its sap. (3) The nucleus of some single-celled organism, *O1*, is destroyed and replaced with a [transplanted] nucleus, *N*, from *O2*, a diverse co-specific organism, producing a viable organism. Assuming that *N* is a master-part, **D8** has the plausible consequence that *O1* ceases to exist and *O2* continues to exist.

D8 is inspired by Aristotle's *principium individuationis* for living organisms: their differing *vital parts* (or differing "vital principles").[21] Moreover, **D8** coheres with the Hoffman/Rosenkrantz account of a [carbon-based] living organism's mereological unity described earlier. I conjecture that a [carbon-based] living organism's having a master-part is a Kripkean *a posteriori* necessity about a natural kind.

D8 differs from the *Lockean criterion*, i.e., *x* and *y* are the same living thing just if *x* and *y* have the *same life*, in being *less general* and in *not* referring to the *sameness of lives*. The Lockean criterion avoids vicious circularity *only if* the sameness of lives can be understood independently of the sameness of *living things*. However, because lives appear to be *processes* that essentially involve *changes in living things*, it is unclear that the sameness of lives can be so understood.[22]

---

[21] *Generation of Animals*, book 4, section 4.
[22] Many thanks to Joshua Hoffman, Brad Hooker, E. J. Lowe, Hugh Mellor, and David Oderberg for their insightful comments.

6

CLASSIFYING PROCESSES: AN ESSAY IN APPLIED ONTOLOGY

Barry Smith

Abstract
We begin by describing recent developments in the burgeoning discipline of applied ontology, focusing especially on the ways ontologies are providing a means for the consistent representation of scientific data. We then introduce Basic Formal Ontology (BFO), a top-level ontology that is serving as domain-neutral framework for the development of lower level ontologies in many specialist disciplines, above all in biology and medicine. BFO is a bicategorial ontology, embracing both three-dimensionalist (continuant) and four-dimensionalist (occurrent) perspectives within a single framework. We examine how BFO-conformant domain ontologies can deal with the consistent representation of scientific data deriving from the measurement of processes of different types, and we outline on this basis the first steps of an approach to the classification of such processes within the BFO framework.[1]

1. The Background of Applied Ontology

1.1 Applied Ontologies in Biology

In the wake of the successful sequencing of the human genome, contemporary biology has been transformed into a discipline in which computer processing of genomic data plays an essential role. But genomic data processed by computers are useful to our understanding of, say, animal behavior, or human health and disease, only if some way can be found to link these data to theoretical assertions using terms that are intelligible to biologists. Such links are created by means of what biologists call

---

[1] With acknowledgements to all of those who have worked on the development of Basic Formal Ontology since its inception, and with special thanks to Thomas Bittner, Werner Ceusters, Damiano Costa, Pierre Grenon, Ingvar Johansson, Kevin Mulligan, Chris Mungall, Alan Ruttenberg, and Peter Simons. The work on this essay was partially supported by the National Institutes of Health through the NIH Roadmap for Medical Research, Grant 1 U 54 HG004028 (National Center for Biomedical Ontology).

'ontologies', which are classifications of biological and other phenomena used to annotate (or 'tag') genomic and other experimental data in a systematic way that enables computers to gain
consistent access even to data that has been collected in highly
heterogeneous ways.[2]
    When scientists are collecting data, this still frequently happens
in a poorly coordinated fashion, and this is so even where the
scientists in question are working in the same field. The data are
in consequence difficult to aggregate in ways that might be useful
in testing hypotheses or in drawing comparisons. In former times
the needed connections were drawn through manual inter-
vention by human beings familiar with the subject-matter. The
indispensability of computers to the processing of data in
information-intensive areas of science, however, has brought the
recognition that ways need to be found to establish such connections computationally. The rise of science-based ontologies[3] is one
product of this recognition.[4]
    We shall focus in what follows on those ontologies that are
being developed on the basis of the assumption that, to create an
ontology that brings benefits to scientists working with data in a
given domain, the ontology should employ classifications that are
based on the established scientific understanding of the entities
and relations in this domain.[5] An ontology of this sort comprises
theoretical terms used to represent the types or classes of entities
in some given domain together with relational expressions representing the relations between these entities. It thereby extends
into the terminology of scientific theories some of the advantages
brought by the International System of Units to the consistent
representation of experimental data expressed in quantitative
terms.
    Each ontology can be conceived as a set of terms (nouns and
noun phrases) which form the nodes of a directed acyclical graph,
as in Figure 1. We can think of the nodes in such a graph as

    [2]   David P. Hill, et al., 'Gene Ontology Annotations: What They Mean and Where They
Come From', *BMC Bioinformatics*, 9 (2008), S2.
    [3]   On May 7, 2012 a google query for 'ontology and database' returned some 10 million
hits, almost twice as many as are returned for the query 'ontology and philosophy'.
    [4]   Judith Blake, 'Bio-ontologies – fast and furious', *Nature Biotechnology* 22 (2004), 773–
774.
    [5]   Some of the principles governing ontologies of this sort are set forth and defended in
Barry Smith and Werner Ceusters, 'Ontological Realism as a Methodology for Coordinated
Evolution of Scientific Ontologies', *Applied Ontology*, 5 (2010), 139–188.

representing *types* or *universals*,[6] which are the sorts of entities represented by the general terms used in formulating scientific theories such as 'cell' or 'electron' and which have *instances* which are the sorts of entities that are observed in scientific experiments. The nodes in the graph are joined by edges representing relations between the types, of which the most important (illustrated in Figure 1) are *is_a* (abbreviating 'is a subtype of') and *part_of*.[7]

Figure 1 Fragments of the Gene Ontology from http://www.ebi.ac.uk/ QuickGO/. Nodes in the graph represent types in reality; edges represent *is_a* and *part_of* relations

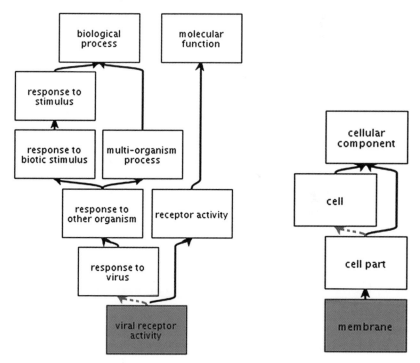

[6] We use these expressions synonymously in what follows. In the wider ontological literature the term 'class' is often used for what we are here calling types or universals.

[7] Barry Smith, et al., 'Relations in Biomedical Ontologies', *Genome Biology* (2005), 6 (5), R46.

When two nodes are joined together by the *is_a* relation, as for example in:

(1) *receptor activity is_a molecular function*

then this represents an assertion to the effect that all instances of the first type are also instances of the second type. When two nodes are joined together by the *part_of* relation, as in

(2) *viral receptor activity part_of response to virus*

then this represents an assertion to the effect that every instance of the first type is a part of some instance of the second type. (Here 'part of' in the unitalicized form represents the familiar instance-level parthood relation holding between, for example, your finger and your hand, or between the first half of a football match and the whole match.[8])

1.2 The Common Logic Interchange Format and the Web Ontology Language

Ontological axioms such as (1) and (2), together with accompanying definitions of terms and relations, are formulated using logical languages – typically fragments of first-order logic – developed to facilitate the representation and interchange of information and data among disparate computer systems.[9] Prominent examples are the (CLIF) Common Logic Interchange Format[10] and the (OWL) Web Ontology Language[11]. Common Logic is an ISO Standard family of languages with an expressivity equivalent to that of first-order logic. OWL-DL is a fragment of the language of first order logic belonging to the family of what are called Description Logics. While OWL-DL is marked by severe restrictions on its expressivity, the theories formulated in its terms have

---

[8]   See again 'Relations in Biomedical Ontologies'.
[9]   http://metadata-stds.org/24707/index.html.
[10] *Common Logic – A Framework for a Family of Logic-Based Languages*, ed. Harry Delugach. ISO/IEC JTC 1/SC 32N1377, International Standards Organization Final Committee Draft, 2005-12-13; http://cl.tamu.edu/docs/cl/32N1377T-FCD24707.pdf.
[11] 'OWL 2 Web Ontology Language', http://www.w3.org/TR/owl2-overview.

desirable computational properties. Because logical languages such as CLIF or OWL are used in their formulation, ontologies themselves can be viewed as simple first-order theories. Providing care is taken to use terms, definitions and relational expressions in consistent ways in different ontologies, such theories can be merged at will to create larger ontologies and, at least in the case of ontologies formulated using a language like OWL, the consistency of such mergers can be checked automatically using dedicated software applications called 'reasoners'.[12]

1.3 The Gene Ontology

It is the Gene Ontology (GO), portions of which are illustrated in Figure 1, which is the most successful ontology currently being used by scientists in reasoning with experimental data.[13] The GO consists of three sub-ontologies, together comprehending some 30,000 terms representing types and subtypes of *biological processes, molecular functions,* and *cellular components.* The GO is used by researchers in biology and biomedicine as a controlled vocabulary for describing in species-neutral fashion the attributes of genes and gene products (for example proteins) identified both in experiments on model organisms such as mouse or fly and in clinical studies of human beings. The GO offers a set of terms, such as 'membrane' or 'viral receptor activity' or 'meiosis', which are defined in ways which reflect the usage of biologists. It thereby provides a means of computationally associating humanly intelligible descriptions of biological phenomena with the massive quantities of sequence data being made available through genomic experimentation. Because the GO is species neutral, it provides a means of comparing data pertaining to different organisms in a way which allows results gained through experimentation on non-human organisms to be exploited in studies of human health and disease.[14]

[12] http://www.w3.org/2007/OWL/wiki/Implementations.
[13] The Gene Ontology Consortium, et al., 'Gene Ontology: Tool for the Unification of Biology', *Nature Genetics*, 2000 May; 25(1): 25–29.
[14] See for example A. Mohammadi et al., 'Identification of Disease-Causing Genes Using Microarray Data Mining and Gene Ontology,' *BMC Medical Genomics*, 2011; 4: 12.

1.4 The Gene Ontology and the Unification of Science

The GO is described by its originators as a 'tool for the unification of biology', and we can see how it is being used, in conjunction with other ontologies such as the Protein[15] and Cell Ontologies[16], to realize at least a part of the old logical empiricist vision of a logical unification of scientific knowledge.[17] One aspect of this realization – not clearly anticipated by the logical empiricists – is the degree to which not only do theoretical assertions need to be unified through use of common logically structured ontologies, but so also do experimental data (for example gene or protein sequence data) compiled in databases processed by computers. In addition, bioinformaticians have discovered that additional ontology resources are needed to unify both of these with assertions about the experimental and computational procedures used to generate the data. This aspect of the unification of science is addressed by the Ontology for Biomedical Investigations (OBI),[18] which comprehends a set of terms which can be used to describe the attributes of experiments in biological and related domains. The goal is a logically well-structured set of preferred terms and logical definitions that can be used to support common access to, and computational reasoning over, data about experiments in order to address the problems which arise at the point where experimental methods (or protocols or statistical algorithms or sample processing techniques or software or equipment used) have become so complex as to cause problems for the interpretation and comparison of the results achieved with their aid. The underlying idea is that use of the OBI vocabulary to annotate results obtained through experimentation would make these results not only more easily interpretable by human beings but also more reliably processable by computers.

[15] Darren A. Natale, et al. 'The Protein Ontology: A Structured Representation of Protein Forms and Complexes', *Nucleic Acids Research*, 39 (2011), D539–45.
[16] Terrence F. Meehan, et al. 'Logical Development of the Cell Ontology', *BMC Bioinformatics* 12 (2011), 6.
[17] Rudolf Carnap, 'Logical Foundations of the Unity of Science', *International Encyclopaedia of Unified Science*, vol. I, Chicago: University of Chicago Press, 1938. Compare also J. J. Woodger, *The Axiomatic Method in Biology*, Cambridge: Cambridge University Press, 1937, and the discussion in Smith and Ceusters, 'Ontological Realism'.
[18] Ryan R. Brinkman, et al., 'Modeling Biomedical Experimental Processes with OBI', *Journal of Biomedical Semantics*, 2010, 1, Suppl. 1.

2. Basic Formal Ontology

As will by now be clear, the principal concerns of applied ontologists are highly practical in nature. Just occasionally, however, they still face problems of a recognizably philosophical sort, and one such problem – relating to the treatment of process measurement data – is the topic of this essay.

Basic Formal Ontology (BFO) is a domain-neutral resource used by biologists and others to provide a top-level ontology that can serve as a common starting point for the creation of domain ontologies in different areas of science.[19] BFO provides a formal-ontological architecture and a set of very general terms and relations that are currently being used by more than 100 ontology development groups in biology and other fields.[20]

BFO is, by the standards predominant in contemporary ontology, very small, consisting of just 34 terms (see Figure 2), including both familiar terms such as 'process', 'object', 'function', 'role' and 'disposition', and less familiar terms such as 'generically dependent continuant' and 'continuant fiat boundary'. Each of these terms must either be declared primitive and elucidated by examples and accompanying axioms, or it must be defined in a logically coherent way in terms of these primitives.

2.1 Continuants and Occurrents

BFO takes as its starting point a familiar distinction between two sets of views, which we can refer to as four-dimensionalist and three-dimensionalist, respectively. Four-dimensionalists (in simple terms) see reality as consisting exclusively of four-dimensional entities (variously referred to as processes, events, occurrents, perdurants, spacetime-worms, and so forth). They thereby regard all talk of entities of other sorts – for example, of three-dimensional things such as you and me – as a mere locution, to be eliminated in favour of some ultimate four-dimensionalist translation. (A four-dimensionalist might hold, for example, that only processes exist, and that talk of continuously existing things pertains rather to special kinds of processual entities, for example

---

[19] http://ontology.buffalo.edu/BFO/Reference.
[20] http://www.ifomis.org/bfo/users.

Figure 2 Draft BFO 2.0 *is_a* Hierarchy[21]

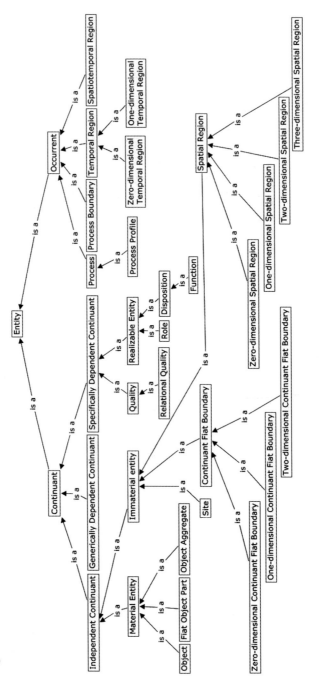

to continuous series of *processes of a bill-clintonizing sort*.[22]) The three-dimensionalists who embrace positions at the opposite extreme see reality as consisting exclusively of entities extended along the three spatial dimensions, and they view all change in terms of the different attributes truly predicable of such entities at different times. Talk of processes, from this perspective, is a mere locution to be eliminated in favour of some ultimate three-dimensionalist translation.

Both families of views bring benefits of their own. In the field of medical ontology, for example, four-dimensionalism provides a natural framework for the ontological treatment of processes of, say, drug interaction or immune response, while three-dimensionalism provides a similarly natural framework for the treatment of the chemical, histological and anatomical structures which participate in such processes.

Unfortunately, the two sets of views are standardly formulated in a way which forces a choice between one or the other. BFO, in contrast, is founded on a bicategorial approach which seeks to combine elements of both the three-dimensionalist and four-dimensionalist perspectives.[23] Thus it incorporates an ontology of continuants and an ontology of occurrents within a single framework in a way that seeks to reconcile the contrasting logico-ontological orders reigning in each.

2.2 Zemach's 'Four Ontologies'

BFO's treatment of the dichotomy between continuants and occurrents is adapted in part from the strategy proposed by Zemach in his 'Four Ontologies'[24] for distinguishing between continuant and non-continuant entities, which Zemach calls 'things' and 'events', respectively. The former, for Zemach, are defined by the fact that they can be sliced (in actuality, or in imagination) to yield parts only along the spatial dimension – for example those parts of your table which we call its legs, top, nails, and so on.[25]

---

[22] W. V. O. Quine, *Word and Object* (Cambridge, MA: The MIT Press), 1960.

[23] Pierre Grenon and Barry Smith, 'SNAP and SPAN: Towards Dynamic Spatial Ontology', *Spatial Cognition and Computation*, 4 (2004), 69–103.

[24] Eddy Zemach, 'Four Ontologies', *Journal of Philosophy* 23 (1970), 231–247.

[25] 'My desk stretches from the window to the door. It has spatial parts, and can be sliced (in space) in two. With respect to time, however, a thing is a continuant.' ('Four Ontologies', p. 240)

The latter, in contrast, can be sliced to yield parts along any spatial and temporal dimensions. For example: the first year of the life of your table; the entire life of your table top (as contrasted with the life of your table legs); and so forth. As Zemach puts it:

> An event is an entity that exists, in its entirety, in the area defined by its spatiotemporal boundaries, and each part of this area contains a *part* of the whole event. There are obviously indefinitely many ways to carve the world into events, some of which are useful and interesting (e.g., for the physicist) and some of which – the vast majority – seem to us to create hodge-podge collections of no interest whatsoever. ('Four Ontologies', pp. 233 f.)

Zemach notes that it is the ontology of continuants that comes most naturally to normal persons:

> We normally regard almost every object we come across as a [continuant entity]: this chair, my pencil, my friend Richard Roe, the tree around the corner, the fly that crawls on the page. [The names we give to chairs and dogs] in our language, obey a grammar which is fundamentally dissimilar to the grammar of names of events. ('Four Ontologies', p. 240)

You, for example, are a continuant; your arms and legs are parts of you; your childhood, however, is not a part of you; rather, it is a part of your life. Continuants are entities which have no parts along the time axis; that is, they may be extended along the three spatial dimensions, not however along the temporal dimension.

It will be important for what follows that BFO generalizes Zemach's idea of a continuant entity by allowing not only *things* (such as pencils and people) as continuants, but also entities that are *dependent* on things, such as qualities and dispositions such as solubility and fragility.[26] The solubility of a given portion of salt requires a dissolving process in order to be realized or manifested. A quality, for BFO, is a dependent continuant that does not require such a process of realization of this sort.

---

[26] As we shall see below, processes, for BFO, are also dependent entities; they depend for their existence on the independent continuant entities which are their participants or on which their participants depend.

BFO departs from Zemach also in its account of occurrent entities. What Zemach refers to as 'events' are in every case the whole content of a spatiotemporal region. As we shall see, however, what BFO 'processes' are conceived in such a way that multiple processes are able to occupy the same spatiotemporal region, as for example when a process of your running down the street is co-located with a process of your getting warmer. The distinction between continuants and occurrents is for BFO categorical. All the parts of continuants are continuants, and any whole to which a continuant belongs is also a continuant. Similarly, all the parts of occurrents are occurrents, and any whole to which an occurrent belongs is also an occurrent. This division flows from two essentially different ways of existing in time. For each continuant, there is some temporal interval during which it *exists*. For each occurrent there is some temporal interval during which it *occurs*. Certainly there are manifold connections between continuants and occurrents, but they are secured in BFO not through parthood relations, but rather through relations of participation.[27]

2.3 The Ontological Square

In allowing not only things but also entities that are dependent on things as continuants, BFO draws on Aristotle's ideas concerning the division of substances and accidents, which reappears in BFO as the division between independent and dependent continuants. Given that BFO accepts also the distinction between universals and particulars, it thus recapitulates Aristotle's ontological square,[28] as represented in Table 1.

2.4 Determinable and Determinate Quality Universals

Qualities are first-class entities in the BFO ontology (of the sort referred to elsewhere in the literature as 'tropes', or 'individual

[27]   Barry Smith and Pierre Grenon, 'The Cornucopia of Formal-Ontological Relations', *Dialectica* 58: 3 (2004), 279–296.
[28]   See Barry Smith, 'Against Fantology', in J. C. Marek and M. E. Reicher (eds.), *Experience and Analysis*, Vienna: HPT&ÖBV, 2005, 153–170. Compare also E. J. Lowe, *The Four-Category Ontology. A Metaphysical Foundation for Natural Science*, Oxford University Press: Oxford 2006, and Luc Schneider, 'Revisiting the Ontological Square', in A. Galton and R. Mizoguchi (eds.), *Formal Ontology in Information Systems, Proceedings of the Sixth International Conference*, Amsterdam: IOS Press, 2010, 73–86.

Table 1: Aristotle's Ontological Square in BFO form

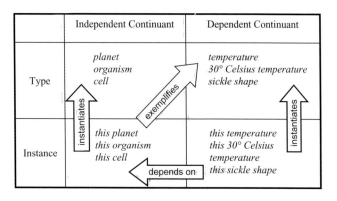

accidents'). They are entities which are dependent on the independent continuant entities (such as molecules, organisms, planets) which are their bearers. Qualities instantiate quality universals, which are divided into *determinable* (such as *temperature, length* and *mass*) and *determinate* (such as *37.0°C temperature, 1.6 meter length,* and *4 kg mass*).[29]

Determinable quality universals are *rigid* in the sense that, if a determinable quality universal is exemplified by a particular bearer at any time during which this bearer exists, then it is exemplified at every such time.[30] John's temperature (a certain quality instance inhering in John from the beginning to the end of his existence) instantiates the same determinable universal *temperature* throughout John's life, even while instantiating different determinate temperature universals from one moment to the next, as illustrated in Figure 3.

We note in passing that the determinate temperature universals are independent of whatever system of units is used to describe them. The universals here referred to in terms of degrees Celsius would be instantiated even in a world in which the Celsius or any other system of units had never been proposed. We note also that for certain families of determinate qualities we can draw a

[29] Ingvar Johansson, 'Determinables are Universals,' *The Monist,* 83 (2000), 101–121.
[30] To say that a quality universal is exemplified by an independent continuant is to say that some instance of this universal is dependent upon (inheres in) this independent continuant as its bearer.

**Figure 3 John's temperature and some of the determinable and deter-
minate universals it instantiates at different times**

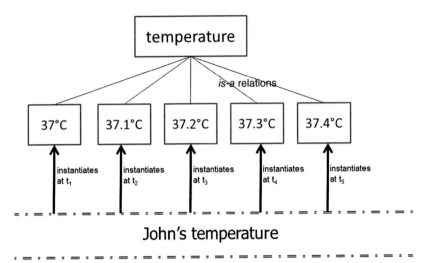

John's temperature

distinction between what we can think of as absolute and relative
values, respectively. The Kelvin scale is a scale of absolute temperature values in this sense.

We can acknowledge also a second sense of 'relative' for determinate qualities that is involved for example when clinicians speak
of temperatures as falling within some 'normal' range. A single
person has a normal temperature in this sense only relative to (the
temperature qualities of) persons in one or other larger population (for example healthy persons at rest in an indoor environment, persons recovering from pneumonia, persons sharing a
certain genetic mutation in common, and so on).

3. Processes in BFO

Our primary concern in the remainder of this essay is with BFO's
treatment of occurrents, which include processes, process boundaries (for example beginnings and endings), spatiotemporal
regions, and temporal intervals and temporal instants. BFO uses
'occupies' to refer to the relation that holds between an occurrent
and the spatiotemporal region which it exactly fills. Processes and
process boundaries *occupy* spatiotemporal regions and they *span*

114   BARRY SMITH

temporal intervals and temporal instants, respectively. Processes are thus distinguished from process boundaries in that the former, but not the latter, are temporally extended.

The assertion that one entity is an occurrent part of a second entity means simply that both are occurrents and that the first is a part – for example a sub-process – of the second. The sum of all processes taking place in your upper body during the course of your life is a proper occurrent part of the sum of processes taking place in your whole body during the same period. There is however a narrower relation which holds between occurrents *a* and *b* in the case where *a* is exactly the restriction of *b* to a temporal region that is a proper part of the temporal region spanned by *b*. When this relation holds, we shall say that *a* and *b* stand in the relation of *temporal parthood*, defined as follows:[31]

a temporal_part_of *b* =Def.
 a occurrent_part_of *b*
  & for some temporal region *r* (*a* spans *r*
   & for all occurrents *c*, *r'*
    if (*c* spans *r'* & *r'* occurrent_part_of *r*)
     then (*c* occurrent_part_of *a* iff *c* occurrent_part_of *b*)))

The first quarter of a game of football is a temporal part of the whole game. The process of your heart beating from 4pm to 5pm today is a temporal part of the entire process of your heart beating throughout your life. The 4th year of your life is a temporal part of your life, as is the process boundary which separates the 3rd and 4th years of your life. The process of a footballer's heart beating once is an occurrent part, but not a temporal part, of the whole game (because when this heart beat occurs many other things are occurring which are also occurrent parts of the whole game).

3.1 BFO's Treatment of Quality Measurement Data

When BFO is used to annotate the results of measurements of qualities, then in a typical case, for example in the case where your height is being measured, the following elements can be distinguished:

[31] Compare Peter M. Simons, *Parts. A Study in Ontology*, Oxford: Clarendon Press, 1987, p. 132.

(1) the BFO:object that is you,
(2) the BFO:quality that is your height,
(3) the BFO:one-dimensional spatial region, stretching at some time t between the top of your head and the base of your feet, that is measured when we measure your height at t.

The result of this measurement is expressed by means of

(4) the BFO:generically dependent continuant expression: '1.7 m tall'.

Each item on this list is unproblematically identifiable as instantiating a BFO category. (4) is an information artifact.[32] It can be stored, for instance, as a record in some file on your laptop. The record is said to be *generically dependent* upon its bearer since it can be transferred to another laptop through a process of exact copying. The temperature of your laptop, in contrast, is *specifically dependent* on the laptop, since a temperature (a specific instance of the universal *temperature*) cannot migrate from one body to another.

3.2 Ontological Treatment of Process Measurements

What happens, now, when we attempt to develop a corresponding analysis in BFO terms of the data resulting from measurements of processes? In the case of a body moving with constant speed, for example, we can here distinguish at least the following elements:

(1) the BFO:object that is moving (changing its spatial location),
(2) the BFO:process of moving (change of spatial location),
(3) the BFO:spatiotemporal region occupied by this process (the path of the motion),
(4) the BFO:temporal region spanned by this process (the temporal projection of (3)),
(5) the speed of the process (rate of change of the spatial location of (1)),

---

[32] http://code.google.com/p/information-artifact-ontology/.

where (5) is represented by means of

(6) the BFO:generically dependent continuant expression: '3.12 meters per second'.

Each of the items (1)–(4) and (6) instantiates a readily identifiable BFO category. For item (5), on the other hand, there is no candidate category in the BFO ontology, since there is no counterpart on the occurrent side for BFO's qualities of independent continuants.[33]

3.3 Why Processes Do Not Change

To see why not, we need to understand the reason why qualities of independent continuants are accepted by BFO as first class entities. This turns on the fact that *independent continuants can change* from one time to the next by gaining and losing qualities. No counterpart of such change can be accepted by BFO on the occurrent side, since it follows trivially from BFO's four-dimensionalist account of occurrents that *occurrents cannot change.*

Processes, in particular, cannot change on the four-dimensionalist view, because processes *are* changes (they are changes in those independent continuant entities which are their participants).[34] Certainly we have ways of speaking whose surface grammar suggests that processes can change. But when we say, for example, *let's speed up this process*, then what we mean (in four-dimensionalist terms) is: let's ensure that some on-going process is one which will be quicker than the process that would have occurred had we not made some specific extra effort.

---

[33] Note that we could view speed in BFO terms as a (non-rigid) quality of the moving object, a view conformant with our way of speaking when we talk, for example, of the speed of light, or the speed of the earth, or the speed of a billiard ball. We believe that a view along these lines for process measurement data in general can and should be developed, since processes of each different type can occur only if there are corresponding types of qualities and dispositions on the side of the continuants which are their participants. Thus we see a view of this sort as a supplement to an account along the lines presented in the text.

[34] Antony Galton and Riichiro Mizoguchi, 'The Water Falls but the Waterfall Does Not Fall: New Perspectives on Objects, Processes and Events', *Applied Ontology*, 4 (2009), 71–107.

Continuants may change not only through change in qualities but also in other ways. For example they may gain and lose parts over time, as for example when you gain and lose cells from your body. To address such changes, BFO's instance-level continuant parthood relation is indexed by time. The counterpart relation on the side of occurrents, in contrast, holds always in a non-indexed way.[35] If a process p_1 occupying temporal interval t_1 is a part of a second process p_2 occupying temporal interval t_2, then p_1 is timelessly a part of p_2 just as t_1 is timelessly a part of t_2.

A second way in which continuants, but not occurrents, may change is by instantiating non-rigid universals. We saw examples of this in our discussion of dependent continuant universals such as temperature above. But examples can be found also among independent continuant universals such as *larva* or *fetus*. If some organism *a* instantiates the universal *larva* at *t*, for example, then it does not follow that *a* instantiates *larva* at all times at which *a* exists. Universals on the side of occurrents, in contrast, are always rigid, so that if an occurrent instantiates a universal at some time, then it instantiates this universal at all times.[36]

An apparent analogue of the phenomenon of non-rigidity in the realm of occurrents is illustrated by a case such as the following. Suppose John, half way through some 20 minute running process *p*, increases his running speed from 6 to 7 mph. Could we not then say that the process *p* instantiates the determinate universal *6 mph running process* in the first 10 minute interval and the determinate universal *7 mph running process* in the second? On the four-dimensionalist view, the answer to this question is 'no': *p* never instantiates the universal *6 mph running process*, any more than the front half of my rabbit instantiates the universal *rabbit*. What we can more properly assert is that *p*, timelessly, has a sub-process p_1 (a temporal part of *p*), which instantiates the universal *6 mph running process*, and a subsequent sub-process p_2 (a second temporal part of *p*) which instantiates the universal *7 mph running process*.

[35] See again Smith, et al., 'Relations in Biomedical Ontologies'.
[36] See again 'Relations in Biomedical Ontologies'.

*3.4 First Approximation to a Solution of the Problem of Process
Measurement Data*

How, then, do we respond to the need on the part of the users of
BFO to annotate data deriving from measurements which have
processes as their targets?

Our response is, in first approximation, very simple: when we
predicate, for instance, 'has speed 3.12 m/s', of a certain process
of motion, then we are asserting, not that that the process in
question *has some special quality* which the same process, in another
scenario, might conceivably have lacked. Rather, we are asserting
that this process *is of a certain special type*. Thus an assertion to the
effect that

(1) motion p has speed v

is analogous, not to:

(2) rabbit r has weight w,

but rather to:

(3) rabbit r instance_of universal *rabbit*.

(1), in other words, should be interpreted as being of the form:

(4) motion p instance_of universal *motion with speed v*.

where the universal *motion with speed v* is a specification of the
universal *motion*.[37]

This treatment of attribution in terms of instantiation reflects
what is standard policy in other parts of BFO in accordance with
its goal of remaining ontologically simple. There are no qualities
of occurrents, in BFO, just as there are no qualities of qualities,
and also no qualities of spatial or temporal regions. Leaving aside
the single case of qualities of independent continuants, attributions in BFO are quite generally treated in terms of the relation of
instantiation, as in Table 2:

---

[37] See Ingvar Johansson, 'Four Kinds of Is_a Relation', in Katherine Munn and Barry
Smith (eds.), *Applied Ontology*, Frankfurt/Lancaster: ontos, 2008, 269–293.

Table 2: Examples of attributions in BFO

spatial region *r* has volume *w*	*r* instance_of universal *region with volume w*
height quality *q* has value 2 meters at *t*	*q* projects onto a one-dimensional spatial region *r* at *t* and *r* instance of universal *2 meter long one-dimensional spatial region*
temporal region *t* has duration *d*	*t* instance_of universal *temporal region with duration d*
temperature quality *q* has value 63° Celsius	*q* instance_of universal *63° Celsius temperature quality*
process *p* has duration *d*	process *p* spans temporal region *t* and *t* instance_of universal *temporal region with duration d*
motion *p* of object *o* has trajectory with shape *s*	the sequence of locations occupied by object *o* at successive instants of time forms a spatiotemporal region *t* and *t* instance_of universal *spatiotemporal region with shape s*

3.5 Processes as Dependent Entities

Processes themselves stand to the independent continuants which are their participants in a relation that is analogous to that in which qualities stand to the independent continuants which are their bearers. In both cases we have to deal with the relation of what BFO calls *specific dependence*.[38] This means that we can extend the ontological square in Table 1 with a representation of the relation between instances and universals on the side of occurrents to create an ontological sextet, as in Table 3.[39]

Our strategy, now, is to use the instantiation relation captured in the rightmost column of Table 3 as basis for an account of the truthmakers of process attributions. But to make an approach along these lines work, certain problems still need to be addressed.

---

[38] See again Smith and Grenon, 'Cornucopia'.
[39] See again Smith, 'Against Fantology'.

Table 3: The Ontological Sextet

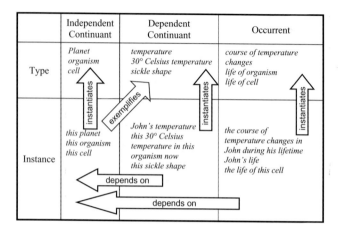

4. Process Profiles

We note, first, that a single running process *p* might be an instance of multiple determinable universals such as:

running process
constant speed running process
cardiovascular exercise process
air-displacement process
compression sock testing process

as well as of multiple determinate universals such as

running process of 30 minute duration
3.12 m/s motion process
9.2 calories per minute energy burning process
30.12 liters per kilometer oxygen utilizing process

and so on.

How, given the complexity of this list and of the many similar lists which could be created for many other types of process, are we to create classifications of the process universals instantiated in different domains in the sort of principled way that will be necessary to ensure consistency and interoperability when classifications are needed for the annotation of data in domains such as physiology or pathology?

To see the lines of our answer to this question, consider Figure 4, which illustrates the cardiac events occurring in the left ventricle of a human heart. This figure tells us that each successive beating of the heart is such as to involve multiple different sorts of physiological processes, corresponding to measurements along the six distinct dimensions of *aortic pressure, atrial pressure, ventricular pressure, ventricular volume, electrical activity,* and *voltage*[40], respectively.[41]

Figure 4 A Wiggers diagram, showing the cardiac processes occurring in the left ventricle[42]

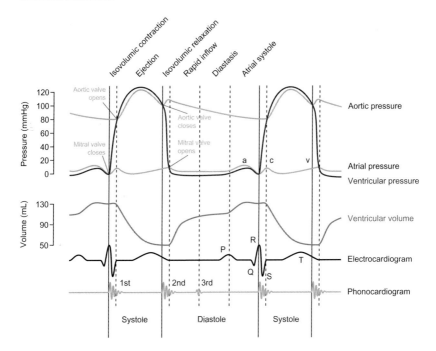

---

[40] Here voltage is used as a proxy for the intensity of sound.

[41] As de Bono, et al., point out, these measurements reflect the variables encoded in models of human physiology created by scientists using ordinary differential equations (Bernard de Bono, Robert Hoehndorf, et al., 'The RICORDO Approach to Semantic Interoperability for Biomedical Data and Models: Strategy, Standards and Solutions', *BMC Research Notes* 4 (2011), 31).

[42] Cardiac Cycle, Left Ventricle, http://commons.wikipedia.org/wiki/File:Wiggers_Diagram.svg.

These structural dimensions are, equivalently, different dimensions along which processes can be compared. When comparing two heart beating processes as being for example of the *same rate*, or when comparing two games of chess as consisting of the *same series of moves*, then there is something in each of the two processes which is – not numerically but qualitatively – 'the same'. This something which the two processes share in common we shall refer to in what follows to as a *process profile*.

What they share in common more precisely is that each contains an instantiation of the same *process profile universal*. The figure illustrates multiple instantiations of multiple process profile universals reflecting the fact that we can measure and compare cardiac processes along multiple different axes, each of which corresponds, in our proposed terminology, to a different determinable process profile universal.

In the *running* case, similarly, we can measure and compare along different structural dimensions pertaining to *speed of motion, energy consumed, oxygen utilized,* and so forth. In each case we focus on some one structural dimension and thereby ignore, through a process of selective abstraction, all other dimensions within the whole process.

Not every dimension of comparison between processes corresponds to a determinable process profile universal in the sense here intended. When we compare processes as to their duration, for example, or as to the time at which they occur or their trajectory in space and time, then we can advert simply to the temporal or spatiotemporal regions which the processes occupy (see again Table 2 above). We can compare processes also for example in terms of whether they involve the same participants, or take place in the same spatial regions. Process profiles enter into the picture only where it is something (thus some occurrent entity) *in the processes themselves* that serves as *fundamentum comparationis*.

4.1 Quality Process Profiles

The simplest example of a process profile is that part of a process which serves as the target of selective abstraction focused on a sequence of instances of determinate qualities such as temperature or height. When we measure, for example, the *process of temperature increase* in patient John, then there is a sequence of determinate temperature qualities whose values when measured on some scale are recorded on John's temperature chart. Process profiles of this simple sort can very often be represented by means of a graph in which measures of a certain quality are plotted against time.

4.2 Rate Process Profiles

On a somewhat higher level of complexity are what we shall call rate process profiles, which are the targets of selective abstraction focused not on determinate quality magnitudes plotted over successive instants of time, but rather on certain ratios between these magnitudes and associated intervals of elapsed time. A speed process profile, for example, is represented by a graph plotting against time the ratio of distance covered per unit of time. Since rates may change, and since such changes, too, may have rates of change, we have to deal here with a hierarchy of process profile universals at successive levels, including:

speed profile
   constant speed profile
     2 mph constant speed profile
     3 mph constant speed profile
  acceleration profile (increasing speed profile)
   constant acceleration profile
     32 ft/s² acceleration profile
     33 ft/s² acceleration profile
   variable acceleration profile
     increasing acceleration profile

and so on.

The types and subtypes listed here are in some respects analogous to the determinable and determinable types and subtypes of qualities recognized by BFO-conformant ontologies on the continuant side discussed already in our discussion of Figure 3 above. And here, too, the reader must bear in mind that the determinate process profile universals in question – while they need to be referred to in reporting results of measurement acts using specific units of measure – are in and of themselves unit-specification independent.

Measurement data representing rates are often expressed in terms not of the process profile instantiated across a temporal interval, but rather of what holds at some specific temporal instant. The latter is then defined in terms of the former in the following way:

(1) John is moving with speed v at time instant t

asserts, roughly, that there is some temporal interval (t_1, t_2), including t in its interior, in which the speed v process profile universal is instantiated. More precisely (in order to take account of the fact that John may be moving with a continuously changing speed in the neighborhood of t), (1) must be formulated in something like the following terms:

> (2) Given any ε, however small, we can find some interval (t_1, t_2), including t in its interior, during which the speed w at which John is moving is such that the difference between w and v is less than ε.[43]

4.3 Cyclical Process Profiles

One important sub-family of rate process profiles is illustrated by cyclical processes, for example the 60 beats per minute beating process of John's heart, or the 120 beats per minute of his drumming process, and so on.

Cyclical process profiles are a subtype of rate process profiles in which the salient ratio is not distance covered but rather number of cycles per unit of time. Here again we find a variety of more specialized universals at lower levels of generality, including for example:

rate process profile
   cyclical process profile
      regular cyclical process profile
         3 bpm cyclical process profile
         4 bpm cyclical process profile
      irregular cyclical process profile
         increasing cyclical process profile

and so on.

In the case of a regular cyclical process profile, a rate can be assigned in the simplest possible fashion by dividing the number of cycles by the duration of the temporal region occupied by the process profile as a whole. Irregular cyclical process profiles, for example as identified in the clinic, or in a morse code transmission,

---

[43] ε, v and w are assumed to be measured in some common unit of velocity.

or in readings on an aircraft instrument panel, may be of specific interest because they are of diagnostic or forensic significance.

5. Conclusion: Towards an Ontology of Time Series Graphs

We have dealt in the foregoing with only a small selection of the ways in which processes can be classified through division into types and subtypes. One important next step will deal with the ways in which such classification is complicated by the fact that processes are embedded within a series of larger process wholes, each nested within yet larger process wholes. Thus when a billiard ball is moving across a table, we can focus on the ball's motion relative to the table, but we can also focus on the larger process which is the motion of the body-table system relative to the motion of the earth; or we can focus on the motion of the body-table-earth system relative to the movement of the sun; and so forth.

Human physiological processes, too, are embedded within series of larger wholes in this way. When studying the heart, for example, physiologists may investigate processes within the interior of the left ventricle, interactions between the left ventricle and other parts of the cardiovascular system, interactions between this system and other bodily systems, and so on. Physiologists may be interested in the processes involving multiple organisms; for example they may be interested in some given organism as part of one or other larger whole which includes some population of organisms of a relevant similar type (all humans, all human babies of a given birth weight, all athletes, and so on). *Normal processes* are defined for this larger population (as *normal qualities* were defined above), and deviations from this norm are defined for the single organism relative thereto.

A further application of the theory of process profiles will include the development of an ontology of time series graphs in terms of a view of process profiles as the truthmakers for such graphs. On this basis we will then explore how the ontology of process profiles might throw light on the semantics of differential equations and of the various mathematical models of dynamic systems in physics, biology and other disciplines constructed on their basis.[44]

---

[44] Exploratory work along these lines is described in Daniel L. Cook, et al. 'Physical Properties of Biological Entities: An Introduction to the Ontology of Physics for Biology,' *PLoS ONE*, 2011, 6(12): e28708.

We will investigate also how the theory can be applied not merely to quantitative information artifacts but also to other sorts of symbolic representations of processes, as for instance when a chess game is represented in one or other of the standard chess notations, or when a symphony performance is represented in a score. Interestingly, this score itself serves also to provide the set of instructions for the unfolding performance, and we shall explore also ways in which the idea of process profiles may help to throw light on how such planned processes depend on, and are at the same represented by, the plans or protocols which define them.

INDEX

animate beings 4, 79
  carbon-based organisms 4, 79–80,
    83, 84, 85, 86, 89, 90, 94, 96–9
  central nervous system 96–7
  collectives 82
  death and 84–5
  goal-directed activity 4, 81–2, 87,
    88–94
  mereological unity 82, 99
  metabolic activity 4, 85, 86, 87, 92,
    93, 94
  natural kinds and ontological
    categories 82–5
  non-mental life 85, 86
  non-physical souls 80
  psychological activity 4, 80, 81, 82,
    86, 87
  reproductive activity 85, 86, 92, 93
  suspended animation 94–6
animism 80
applied ontology
  biology 101–4
  Common Logic Interchange
    Format 104, 105
  Gene Ontology 103, 105–6
  process profiles 120–2
    cyclical process profiles 124–5
    quality process profiles 122–3
    rate process profiles 123–4
    time series graphs 125–6
  Web Ontology Language 104–5
  see also Basic Formal Ontology
Aristotle 1, 2, 3, 4
  categorical ontology 7, 10, 11–18,
    82, 99

modal categories 11, 12, 13, 15,
    17, 72–7
  ontological square 111, 112
Armstrong, David 26, 33, 36
artifacts 90–1, 93
artificial boundaries 42
artificial life 87
attributes 17, 18, 19
  see also properties
Austin, J. L. 31

Basic Formal Ontology 107
  continuants 107–12, 116, 117
  determinable and determinate
    quality universals 111–13, 117
  occurrents 107–9, 111, 116, 117
  ontological square 111
  processes 113–14
    change and 116–17
    dependent entities 119–20
    ontological treatments of process
      measurements 115–16
    treatment of quality
      measurement data 114–15,
      118–19
  Zemach's 'Four Ontologies'
    109–11
biology
  applied ontology 101–4
  carbon-based organisms 4, 79–80,
    83, 84, 85, 86, 89, 90, 94, 96–9
  cardiac events 121–2
  central nervous system 96–7
  essentialism 3
  Gene Ontology 103, 105–6

Classifying Reality, First Edition. Edited by David S. Oderberg. Copyright © 2013 The Authors. Book
compilation © 2013 Blackwell Publishing Ltd.

metabolism 4, 85, 86, 87, 92, 93, 94
processes 4, 105
  see also processes
proteinoid microspheres 92–3
pseudoplasmodium 98
species classification 1–2, 17
viruses 86–7
  see also evolutionary biology
Bradley, F. H. 30

carbon-based organisms 4, 79–80, 83,
    84, 85, 86, 89, 90, 94, 96–9
cardiac processes 121–2
categorical predication
  Aristotelian categorical ontology 7,
    10, 11–18, 82, 99
    modal categories 11, 12, 13, 15,
      17, 72–7
    ontological square 111, 112
  category mistake 13, 16, 91
  existence 9, 16, 20
  formally correct statements 20–2
  identity 16
  inherence 11, 14, 15
  object/property distinction 6–10
  particular attributes 12, 17, 26, 28,
    30, 31–2, 37, 39
  predicables 12, 14, 19
  quantifiers 16, 28, 29, 30, 31, 37
  relational predicates 6, 19
  substance 11, 13, 14, 15, 16, 17, 19
  universal attributes 12, 16, 17, 33
causal properties 25, 32, 33, 36, 37
causal relations 63
central nervous system 96–7
change 116–17
class membership 30
classificatory schemes 51–9
  processes see processes
  taxonomy 61–2
colour 30, 33
Common Logic Interchange 104,
    105
conjunctive properties 36–7
continuants 107–12, 116, 117
contrastive explanations 3, 62–8

conventionalism 2, 3, 41–4
  challenges to 44–51, 59–60
counterfactual reasoning 71

Davidson, Donald 33
Dawkins, Richard 87
De Morgan, Augustus 36
death 84–5
Dennett, Daniel 62
developmental programmes 74, 76
disjunctive properties 35, 40
dualism 82
Dummett, Michael 42, 43, 49
Dupré, John 42

electron configuration 45, 46, 47, 49
empirical observations 53, 54, 56
epistemology 3, 70–1, 72, 73
essentialism 3, 49, 74
evolutionary biology
  adaptive value 71–2
  cognitive capacity and 72
  contrastive explanations 3, 62–8
  developmental programmes 74, 76
  impossibilities 63–4, 65, 73, 75–6
  modal categories 65, 69–72
    Aristotelian theses and 72–7
  morphospace 64–5, 68, 76
  neo-Darwinians 65, 66, 67, 76
  organismal design and adaptation
    64
  taxonomy 61–2
  Tree of Life 63, 69
existence 9, 16, 20

Fantology 5, 10, 11
fiat entities 42, 43, 45, 47–8, 49
Fox, Sidney 92
Frege, Gottlob 2, 6, 8, 9, 10, 13,
    26–7, 28, 30, 31
functions 27, 31

Gene Ontology 103, 105–6
genetics 74
genomic data 101–2
Gestalt factors 50, 51, 53

Ghirardi-Rimini-Weber (GRW) theory
    50
goal-directed activity 4, 81–2, 87, 88–94
God 88, 89
Gould, Stephen J. 65, 76
GRW (Ghirardi-Rimini-Weber) theory
    50

hybrids 51–3

idealism 82
identity 16
    mind-independent identity
        conditions 41, 42, 43, 44
individuation 29
inherence 11, 14, 15

Jackson, Frank 30

laws of nature 29, 32–5, 39–40, 46–7
Lewis, David 24, 25, 26, 29, 36, 38–40
Lewis, Peter J. 50
Lima-de-Faria, Antonio 65–7
living things see animate beings;
    biology
Locke, John 99
logical formalism 2, 5, 10, 13, 18

materialism 82
McGhee, G. R. 63, 68
memes 87
Mendeleev, Dmitri 53–4, 57
metabolism 4, 85, 86, 87, 92, 93, 94
mind-independent identity
    conditions 41, 42, 43, 44
modal categories 11, 12, 13, 15, 17
    evolutionary biology 65, 69–72
    Artistotelian theses and 72–7
molecules 46, 47
Moore, G. E. 23, 24, 25, 26
Mumford, Stephen 39

natural boundaries 2–3, 41
    challenges to the conventionalist
        thesis 44–51, 59–60
    classificatory schemes 51–9

conventionalist objections to 41–4
    empirical observations and 53, 54,
        56
    fiat entities and 42, 43, 45, 47–8,
        49
    Gestalt factors and 50, 51, 53
    hybrids and 51–3
    laws of physics 46–7
    macroscopic objects 45, 46, 48–51
    mind-independent identity
        conditions 41, 42, 43, 44
    psychological biases and 3, 51, 54,
        55, 57, 59
natural laws 29, 32–5, 39–40, 46–7
natural properties 2, 24–5, 38–40
natural selection 64, 65, 87
necessary properties 20, 24

occurrents 107–9, 111, 116, 117
Oliver, Alex 28
ontological square 111
ontology 2, 4
    Aristotelian categorical ontology 7,
        10, 11–18, 82, 99
    modal categories 11, 12, 13, 15,
        17, 72–7
    ontological square 111, 112
    see also categorical predication
    object/property distinction 6–10
    predicate logic and 5–6
    see also applied ontology; Basic
        Formal Ontology
Ontology for Biomedical
    Investigations 106

particular attributes 12, 16, 17, 26,
    28, 30, 31–2, 39
Pauli Exclusion Principle 46, 47
periodic table 53–4, 56, 57, 74
persistence conditions 58
plants 98
Plato 25
predicables 12, 14, 19
predicate logic 5–6
predication see categorical
    predication

predictive power 54, 55, 56
processes 4, 105, 113–14
  change and 116–17
  dependent entities 119–20
  ontological treatment of process
    measurement 115–16
  profiles 120–2
    cyclical process profiles 124–5
    quality process profiles 122–3
    rate process profiles 123–4
    time series graphs 125–6
  treatment of quality measurement
    data 114–15, 118–19
properties 2, 11
  causal properties 25, 32, 33, 36,
    37
  colour 30, 33
  conjunctive properties 36–7
  disjunctive properties 35, 40
  first-order/second-order 6, 7, 8,
    9–10, 17–18, 28, 32, 37
  function and 27, 31
  language-independent things 26,
    33, 36, 40
  natural laws and 29, 32–5
  natural properties 2, 24–5, 38–40
  necessary properties 20, 24
  object/property distinction 6–10
  objections to 25–31
  particulars and 12, 16, 17, 26, 28,
    30, 31–2, 37, 39
  Ramsey's test 34–8
  temperature 29, 30, 38, 39, 112,
    113
  universals and 12, 16, 17, 26, 33
    determinable and determinate
      quality universals 111–13, 117
proteinoid microspheres 92–3
pseudoplasmodium 98
psychological activity 4, 80, 81, 82,
    86, 87
  e also animate beings
  ological biases 3, 51, 54, 55, 57,
    9
    Hilary 25, 26, 30, 42

quantifiers 16, 28, 29, 30, 31, 37
quantum mechanics 50
Quine, W. V. 2, 6, 7, 8, 9, 28–30, 34,
    37

Ramsey, F. P. 31, 32, 34–8
realist metaphysics 1, 41, 59–60
relational predicates 6, 19
restricted quantifiers 16
Russell, Bertrand 6, 7, 10

Schaffer, Jonathan 40
Shoemaker, Sydney 33, 39
Smith, Barry 5, 42
Social Darwinism 87
species classification 1–2, 17
speed 117, 118
subatomic particles 45, 46, 47, 49
substance 11, 13, 14, 15, 16, 17, 19
suspended animation 94–6

Tarski, Alfred 2, 27–8, 30
taxonomy 61–2
temperature 29, 30, 38, 39, 112, 113
Thompson, D'Arcy 65
time series graphs 125–6
tropes 31, 32, 39, 111

universal attributes 12, 16, 17, 26, 33
  determinable and determinate
    universals 111–13, 117

van Inwagen, Peter 23
Varzi, Achille 42, 43, 44, 50, 51, 59
viruses 86–7

Web Ontology Language 104–5
Wiggers diagram 121
Williamson, Timothy 71
Wittgenstein, Ludwig 21
Wright, Larry 88

Yablo, Stephen 71

Zemach, Eddy 109–11